CRUISING CORK AND KERRY

Graham Swanson

IMRAY LAURIE NORIE & WILSON

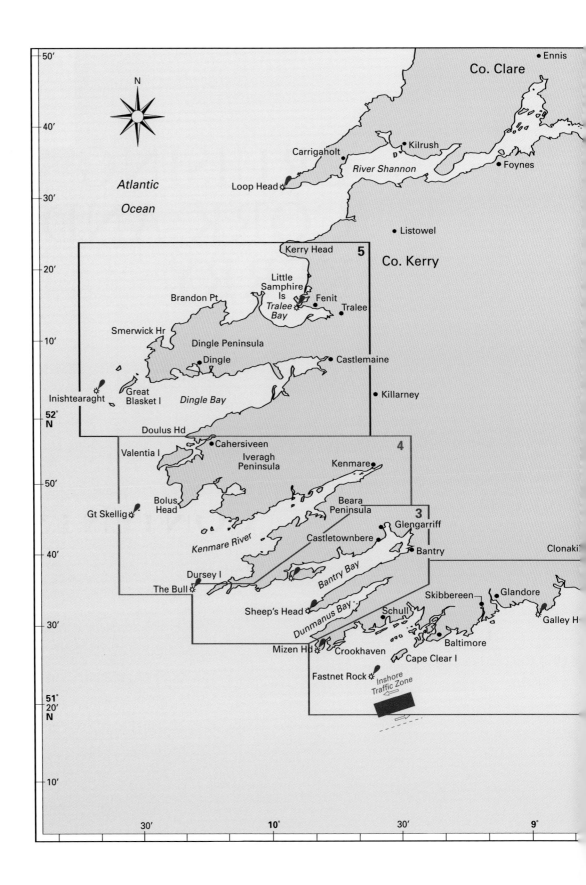

50'

Co. Clare

• Ennis

N

40'

Atlantic

Carrigaholt • Kilrush

30'

Ocean

Loop Head ☼

River Shannon

• Foynes

• Listowel

Kerry Head

5 Co. Kerry

20'

Little
Samphire
Is   • Fenit
Brandon Pt   *Tralee*   • Tralee
              Bay

Smerwick Hr

10'

Dingle Peninsula

• Dingle   • Castlemaine

Inishtearaght

Great
Blaslet I   *Dingle Bay*

• Killarney

**52°
N**

Doulus Hd

4

• Cahersiveen
Valentia I   Iveragh
              Peninsula
                        • Kenmare

50'

Bolus
Head   Beara
                        Peninsula   **3**
Gt Skellig ☼   • Glengarriff
                        Castletownbere • • Bantry   Clonaki

40'

Kenmare River

Dursey I   *Bantry Bay*

The Bull ☼

Skibbereen • Glandore

Sheep's Head ☼   Dunmanus Bay   Schull •   Galley H

30'

Mizen Hd ☼ Crookhaven   • Baltimore
                              Cape Clear I

Fastnet Rock ☼   Inshore
                   Traffic Zone

**51°
20'
N**

10'

30'   10°   30'   9°

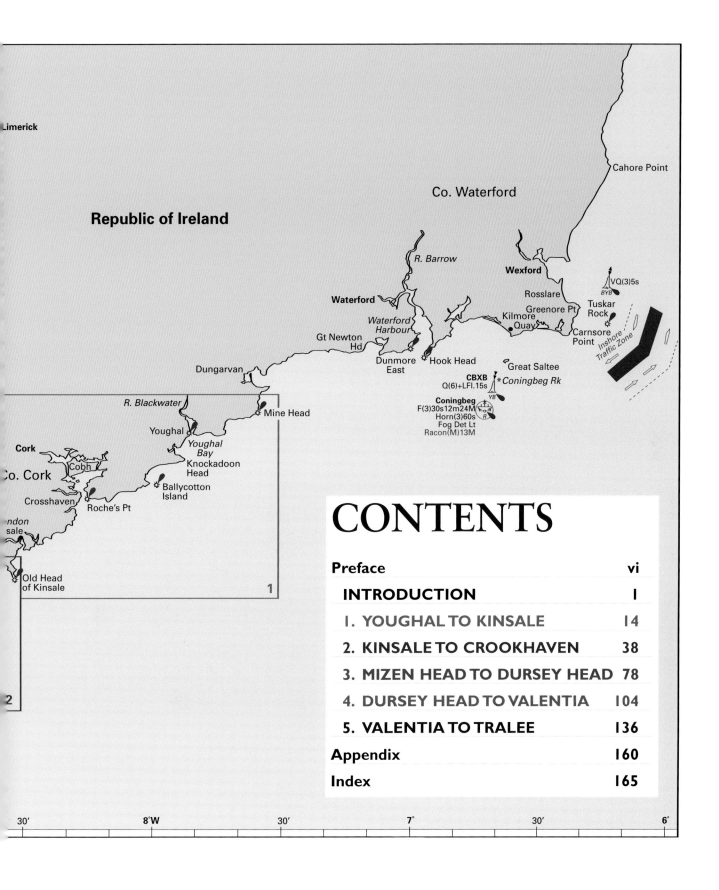

Limerick

Republic of Ireland

Co. Waterford

Cahore Point

R. Barrow

Wexford

Waterford

Rosslare

VQ(3)5s
BYB

Greenore Pt
Kilmore
Quay
*Waterford
Harbour*

Tuskar
Rock

Gt Newton
Hd

Dunmore
East

Hook Head

Carnsore
Point

*Inshore
Traffic Zone*

Dungarvan

Great Saltee

CBXB
Q(6)+LFl.15s

Coningbeg Rk

YB

R. Blackwater

Coningbeg
F(3)30s12m24M
Horn(3)60s
Fog Det Lt
Racon(M)13M

Mine Head

Youghal

*Youghal
Bay*
Knockadoon
Head

Cork

Cobh

Co. Cork

Ballycotton
Island

Crosshaven

Roche's Pt

ndon
sale

Old Head
of Kinsale

1

2

30'   8°W   30'   7°   30'   6°

CONTENTS

Published by
Imray Laurie Norie & Wilson Ltd
Wych House St Ives
Cambridgeshire PE27 5BT England
☎ +44 (0)1480 462114
Fax +44 (0)1480 496109
Email ilnw@imray.com
www.imray.com
2005

1st edition 2005

© Graham Swanson
Graham Swanson has asserted his right to be identified as the author of this work in accordance with the Copyright, Designs and Patents Act 1988.

© Plans Imray Laurie Norie & Wilson Ltd 2005

© Aerial photographs Patrick Roach and Imray Laurie & Wilson Ltd 2005

© Uncredited ground-level photographs Graham Swanson

© Illustrations of sea birds Lucy Wilson 2005

ISBN 0 85288 758 2

British Library Cataloguing in Publication Data.
A catalogue record for this book is available from the British Library.

PLANS
The plans in this guide are not to be used for navigation. They are designed to support the text and should at all times be used with navigational charts.

The plans and tidal information have been reproduced with the permission of the Hydrographic Office of the United Kingdom (Licence No. HO151/951101/01) and the Controller of Her Britannic Majesty's Stationery Office.

CAUTION
Whilst every care has been taken to ensure accuracy, neither the Publishers nor the Author will hold themselves responsible for errors, omissions or alterations in this publication. They will at all times be grateful to receive information which tends to the improvement of the work.

CORRECTIONAL SUPPLEMENTS
This pilot book will be amended at intervals by the issue of correctional supplements which will be published on our website www.imray.com and may be downloaded free of charge. Printed copies are also available on request from the publishers at the above address.

Printed in Singapore

FOREWORD

The waters of Cork and Kerry where I sail myself offer some of the best cruising areas in Europe and are also a challenging area for the racing sailor, though perhaps the less said of that in a cruising guide the better. However, the relevance of guiding advice applies to both, because while the cruiser concentrates on the pleasures of exploration, the racing sailor will be a caller to many of the southwestern harbours on passage from one to the other of the many events that crowd the sailing calendars in this area.

To these coastal counties, Graham Swanson has added those of the adjoining southeastern maritime area of Waterford and the Atlantic coastline as it climbs westwards towards the wide and extensive Shannon Estuary. Graham is a man whom I have not met and only been in touch with through his interest in my national maritime radio programme, *Seascapes*, which he knocked across while he was on the sea waves and I on the air version. So it is unusual to be asked to write the foreword from these contacts, but I do so because he made it clear that he was pursuing, with his wife, a determined approach to creating a guide that would complement, not challenge, the existing Irish Cruising Club's sailing directions and this is a wise decision, for one should not rival those who know their own areas best, but one can complement and add to them.

The sailor can never have too much in the way of information about anchorages, harbours of refuge, shelter and rest areas. Graham's book comes about through, firstly, his own sailing explorations, and then being asked to write a cruising guide covering the area from Youghal to the mouth of the Shannon. It provides an extra resource that will rest easily aboard when on passage and deciding on landfall, or on the shelves of home when the summer is planned from the comfort of the fireside.

Tom MacSweeney
Seascapes
July 2005

The quay at Castletownshend

PREFACE

My publisher agreed that this cruising companion should break the mould of the traditional pilot book and so, having traversed these coasts four times – by land, sea, in print and, finally, with Patrick Roach's excellent photographs, I decided to write this book as an extended cruise.

With only two years to research and write this guide, on waters mainly new to us, *Balair* was positioned to East Ferry Marina in Cork in May 2003, my wife, Joy, joining there with our camper van. That summer we made a complete coastal land reconnaissance of harbours and anchorages from Tralee to Youghal, on County Cork's boundary with County Waterford.

There were few special facilities in Southwest Ireland for yachtsmen until the 1980s. During the years of the 'Celtic Tiger' – the boom of the 1990s – many old fishing and steamer quays were renovated and improved with European money. There are now many new slips, mostly with good parking, for those who trail their boats behind a vehicle. Facilities ashore were also created for a growing tourist industry. All this has made Cork and Kerry (an area which is also known as Ivernia) a much more viable cruising area for both local and foreign sailors. The magnificent seascapes and cloud-capped mountains will never change, though much ashore is no longer what postcards depict. (A donkey carrying turf is a rarity now!)

With careful planning and pilotage these are not difficult coasts to sail, provided you wait for suitable weather. Wind direction is immaterial as a tack across any of the bays is short, before going about below rugged cliffs. (I suggest you cruise fairly quickly to the area of your choice, explore as it suits you, then when homeward bound savour other havens as time and weather permit.) Those familiar with the weather of western Britain will find it very similar in Cork and Kerry. Conditions are modified by the same Gulf Stream and the area is affected by the same weather systems; rain and mist are usually followed by lovely days with blue skies and fluffy white clouds. Persistent high pressure to the south tends to bring northerly pollution-free airs so visibility remains good. (In the sailing season the northern coasts of Ireland tend to get the stronger winds.) Tides are generally weak inshore, except around headlands and through sounds, allowing civilised departure times. Each ria (sunken valley) has flood and ebb tides. Summer days are appreciably longer than in southern England and mainland Europe. All harbours, except for the few with a pronounced entrance bar, can be entered on any tide and in most winds. In fact, low water is usually the preferred entry time, when drying dangers show. Irish sea-area forecasts are excellent; they are updated every six hours and frequently promulgated. We prefer solitary anchorages to marinas or moorings, but others may prefer a more gregarious cruising life-style. *Balair* spent 102 nights free of charge at anchor during 870 miles of coasting to 67 havens in Cork and Kerry. No moorings were taken; it was so much quicker and easier to anchor.

My narrative starts in the east and ends at Barrow Harbour (Fenit–Tralee) on the coast of North Kerry. (This is the way we mainly coasted, with ports and harbours described in logical sequence.) Cork and Kerry are divided into five cruising areas, with suggested 'Arrival Ports' where, after a long passage, crews can rest up, clean up, stoke up and be secure in any weather – before making interesting cruises in that and adjoining areas. The coasts and scenery are described, with points of particular interest. Essential facilities for each haven are given, with a brief taster of what it offers. Then pilotage information, if applicable, is followed by a fuller section on things to do locally. Only useful telephone numbers, which may not be readily available, are given. Facilities change frequently so I do not list ephemeral data. Only long-established restaurants and pubs that we have used, or which have been recommended to us by friends, are mentioned (surely the fun of cruising is discovering these for yourself).

Circumnavigators would find the mainly offshore passage of some seventy miles from Baltimore's lovely natural harbour to Fenit Marina in Tralee Bay a pleasant and challenging sail. *Cruising Cork and Kerry* is not aimed particularly at those who 'have no time to stand and stare', as the Welsh poet W H Davies wrote. Nevertheless, they too will find this guide helpful; though it is mainly for those who wish to get a taste of Southwest Ireland by coasting selected parts at a leisurely pace. A good start could be from the ancient port of Youghal in the east, via Cork's great harbour, to historic Kinsale. Further west is the lovely natural fishing harbour and island-ferry port of Baltimore. This would make an ideal 'sally-port' from which to start exploring the five rias (drowned valleys) – including Long Island Sound – of West Cork and Kerry.

Many families have to take holidays together, though some members do not care for long sea passages and have their own things to do in port. There are good air services to Cork and Kerry, with rail and bus links to most parts. Irish Ferries have services to the east and southeast coasts of Ireland from Wales. Swansea Cork Ferries have services from Wales. Brittany Ferries (France) ply between UK (Plymouth), Ireland and Spain. So family members could join ship in Ireland by public transport; even better, by car or motor home. They could then serve as crew transport and be cruise followers from port to port! In the text I also mention suitable touring caravan parks in the area.

To appreciate fully the natural beauty of the hinterland it is necessary to walk and cycle, use the erratic local bus services or travel by car and taxi. Most havens have places of nearby interest, and bicycles can usually be hired in port towns, but renting a car can be difficult and expensive. Sailors from overseas may wish to fly in and charter a boat – from Cork, Kinsale or Valentia. In the days of sail France and Iberia had extensive trade with western Ireland, leading to intermarriage and other bonds. Ireland is also much favoured by sailors from Scandinavia, whence came her first invaders!

Besides guiding Irish sailors and those from Britain and mainland Europe, I also write for the descendants of the millions of Irish people who were forced by poverty (or the English) to take up residence all over the globe. Some may now wish to cruise the shores that their ancestors left behind forever. You will read and hear much about the Great Famine of the mid-19th century, when the potato crop (the staple food of the poor) failed, thousands died and thousands more emigrated. Before this many had already left Ireland when the fishing industry declined. There were many Anglo-Irish families, some planted originally by the English, who were also forced – one way or another – to emigrate or return to Britain. Those with ancestors who took Ireland's part in her struggles for independence may wish to see where these heroes won or fell. The descendants of all will find much of nostalgic interest in Cork and Kerry.

I am also very interested in the more recent history of Ireland and in the way of life and traditional cooking of the friendly population. This all makes exploring towns, villages, churches and the many old burial grounds much more interesting, and many streets, bridges, buildings, etc. are named after Irish patriots.

My main aim is to enable a cruise to be planned and then enjoyed by all the ship's company. I wish all cruisers, whatever their interests, fair sailing around the shores of County Cork and County Kerry. Please send your comments and corrections by email to: graham.swanson1@tiscali.co.uk and these will be incorporated, as appropriate, in the publisher's website.

Graham Swanson
Gweek, Helston, Cornwall
August 2005

ACKNOWLEDGEMENTS

Besides those named below there must be a hundred more who freely passed on their knowledge in harbours or ashore. Special thanks must go to the following, who enabled us to complete our reconnoitres by land and sea.

Repairman Pat of Cóbh who dropped everything to replace the side-door of our camper van. It took a couple of hours but he would not take a single euro! Boat builder Frank Kowalski (whose stationary(!) Nissan took the door off) for only being slightly annoyed, because his Navara was brand new. The mechanic from Waterville who rescued us when the accelerator cable broke in Darrynane. He ingeniously fixed the engine to run at sufficient speed to get us to his garage – mainly in bottom gear! Kevin Higgins of Marine Motors Ltd, who revived our outboard motor, and David O'Brien for repairing *Balair*'s starter motor. Manager Colm O'Connor of Dunmast Ltd who came out to Kinsale to repair my autohelm, and the kind man there who repaired my Bretton Plotter. Oldcourt Boatyard (and the engineer with the big spanner) who gave me a free berth whilst I repaired *Balair*'s exhaust pipe. The late Concubhor O'Driscoll, master and owner of Cape Clear Island Ferry, on whose bridge I travelled on my first visit to the island. Matt Murphy, who owns Sherkin Island Marine Station.

Harbourmasters Michael McCarthy (Cork City); Phil Devitt (Kinsale); John Minihane (Union Hall); Diarmuid Minihane (Baltimore); Kris Dennisson (Castletownbere); Alec O'Donovan (Bantry Harbour); Brian Farrel (Dingle) and Michael O'Carroll (Fenit). The Coastguard Radio officers I communicated with at Dublin MRCC and Valentia MRSC. It was nice to meet or have telephone conversations with Maurice, Denny, Matt, Russell and Timothy at Valentia MRSC. They all kept track of *Balair* and ensured that I was never out of touch with home base, often arranging link calls.

Arthur Baker, of *Irish Mist* (past Commodore ICC), who radioed with helpful advice when *Balair* was stormbound in West Cove; Captain Robert McCabe – Irish lights, Tom MacSweeney (Marine Correspondent, RTÉ), who broadcast several times on our behalf.

Anne Kelly and Paul Murphy, Kinsale YC & Marina; Johnny Murphy, Dingle Marina; Phil, Fionnuala and Robert Harrington, Lawrence Cove Marine; Carolyn King, Cahersiveen Marina.

For their kindness and help thanks also to Myrtle Allen; David Buttimore; Gráinne Nt Chonchuir; John Christian; Simone Collins; Andrew Cooke; Donal Curran; Brian and Barbira (Dingle); Frank Donaldson; Philip Eden; Paul Elphics; Eddie English; Michael Folly; Patrick Gallagher; Mary Gibbons; Hennie and Willem Giesberts; Mike Haberline; Emma Hargreaves; Erik Haugaard; Catherine and Tom Healy; Jackie Hooley; Alwyn and Mary James; Peter Lambie; Pat Lake; Des and Pat Lavelle; John Leonard; Mrs Levi (Ballydehob); Susan and Michael Loughane; Mary Mackie; Adrienne MacCarthy; Craig McKechnie; Vincent McMahon; 'Sam' and Anne Mearns; Helen Moriarty; Wally Morrissey and daughter Lesley; Aidan O'Connor; Colm O'Connor; Stephen Odlum; Fr O'Donaghue; Donal O'Donovan; Esther O'Donovan; James O'Donovan; Donal O'Driscoll; James O'Driscoll; Kevin O'Farrel; John O'Reagan; Dermot O'Sullivan; Patrick O'Sullivan; Judith and David Pentreath; John Petch; Richie Power; Raymond Ross; Paddy and Francis Sheahan with Paddy and Mary – The Arundel, Kitchen Cove; Ian Sheridan; Edward Twomey; Michael Treacy; Martin Wakefield; Albert and Kitty Walker; Mr and Mrs Eugene Wiseman. We look forward to meeting most of you again when we are updating the guide.

Assistance from Swansea Cork Ferries, Irish Ferries and Air Wales was much appreciated, as was a great deal of help from Cork Kerry Tourism. Without Joy's organisation of all our travel arrangements, particularly our joint initial reconnaissance by land, you would not be reading this. She then had to put my ancient PC copy into Word (not without some discussion!)

Finally, and not least, I am very indebted to Willie Wilson for giving me a free hand, and then, with Alison and the Imray editorial staff, making sense of it all.

Graham Swanson
Helford
August 2005

Dedication

It is appropriate that this guide is dedicated to the late Jim Butler. Jim was an active cruising and racing member of the Irish Cruising Club. Without the marina he designed and built at East Ferry we would never have had such a convenient, convivial and safe base for our boat. Without the Irish *Cruising Club's Sailing Directions* I could not have negotiated all the harbours and almost all the anchorages around the coasts of Cork and Kerry. Jim's widow Margaret and son George were very kind to us, as were Michael and his staff at the marina's Marlogue Inn.

The author, Graham Swanson, at work on *Balair*

INTRODUCTION

GEOGRAPHY AND GEOLOGY

Those who set out to cruise this area thoroughly should have some idea of how the beautiful land and seascapes of Southwest Ireland evolved. First study relatively-small Ireland's location in relation to Great Britain, preferably on a geological map. Then visualise South and Southwest Ireland being once attached to Southwest Wales and England's West Country. Over millions of years layers of sediment settled onto the bed of a then-tropical sea, to be compressed into 1,000 feet of the geologist's old red sandstone. To the layman this is mainly slate, varying in colour between brown, grey and red – as the pebbles on any strand will show. Violent subterranean shifts then lifted the rock of what was to become Southwest Ireland into contorted ridges running mainly west-southwest into the Atlantic. Retreating ice later ground these into smooth mountainous ridges. The valleys in between, which we now know as Bantry Bay, Kenmare River, Dingle Bay and so on, were flooded by the rising sea level. Trees flourished and stabilised the soil, left by the ice, over much of the land. Homo sapiens later cleared most of the trees for building, fuel and agriculture. Subsequent rains eroded much of this soil, leaving the bare mountains of today.

The rias are only a few miles wide and about 10 to 25 miles long. Long Island and Roaring Water Bays were once sunken valleys too. Fastnet Rock would have been the Cape of Ivernia's already dissected little finger – Cape Clear and Sherkin Islands with the islands and mainland north of Baltimore. The strings of islands which lie between Cape Clear Island and the Mizen Peninsula will eventually become reefs. The nearly vertical but relatively soft strata of the Cork and Kerry coasts gets a continual battering before slipping into the sea. There are many 'see through' caves, notably in the Old Head of Kinsale, which one day will form more rocky islands. Currents and waves have also carved great bays in Southwest Ireland's coastal moraine and rock. Further erosion has made these once-natural harbours into havens protected only by islands and rocks.

These rias were important waterways before roads were developed. Goods and passengers travelled to and from the towns at the head of each by sea and a steamer service was eventually established. Most of the old steamer-quays are still in use by fishermen and pleasure craft.

Sailing from Milford Haven through the off-lying Sounds, the contorted rock formations and nasty reefs are similar to those of Southwest Ireland. Cliffs like those below St Ann's Head at the Haven's entrance, layered red and white, can also be seen in Cork and Kerry. The slate of West Cork is like that of Cornwall, which, apart from some very old granite and serpentine, is also old red sandstone. Cornwall's offshore rocks share the name Carrick or Carreg with other Celtic lands, indicating a more recent cultural link.

Ireland was ice-bound long after the land-bridges between mainland Europe, Britain and Ireland had eroded. Thus Ireland has less species of flora and fauna than its neighbours, but because of its non-industrial past it still has many that are not yet extinct. Wild birds in particular are often quite indifferent to the proximity of humans. Red squirrels, rare in southern Britain now, are common in the woods of East Cork.

Watch towers and castles

The coasts of South and West Ireland have many old towers and castles. The towers were for spotting invaders and communication. Fast naval packets often brought the first news of Nelson's battles and the state of play in the American wars to Ireland's southern shores, to be forwarded to London by manual and later electric telegraph. The superior accommodation for the old Coast Guard sometimes had a look-out tower, notably at Courtmacsherry and Crosshaven. Castles were for coastal or personal defence. Only towers and castles which are good aids to navigation or are of particular interest will be mentioned.

Many burial grounds are inside ruined churches

Signs for Kilmalkedar Church near Ballydavid, Smerwick Harbour

Cahersiveen

Portmagee

County Kerry

The Gaeltacht

Parts of counties Kerry and Cork, as well as other counties on Ireland's western seaboard, form an area known as the Gaeltacht, where the language and lifestyle are Gaelic and the government encourages the preservation of Gaelic traditions and active use of the Irish language.

Place names

Place names in this guide are given as on charts and OSI maps, followed by phonetic pronunciation (when known). Some port towns combine a local historic surname with that of the harbour, but spellings can be inconsistent.

On charts and in pilot books words for an island are: Inish, Ennis, Innis, Inis (pronounced 'Inish'), Illan and Illaun. Oileán is a separate word for island and Garnish and Garanish both mean 'near island'. Tra is a strand or beach, Bally a town, Kill a church. Reen and Rinn both mean peninsula or headland – hence the 'Ring' of Kerry for tourists! Knock means hill; Slieve is a mountain. Castle and fort names start with Caher, Dun and Doon. These can vary from the real thing to a small fortified house.

THE BOAT

A reliable engine is needed to negotiate some of the anchorages safely. A fender board, possibly a couple of old tyres, and a ladder will be useful as there are quays – ancient and modern – to lie against. A large boat is not necessary provided it can accommodate the crew comfortably and can carry provisions, reserve water and fuel to keep the ship operational for a week or more. *Balair*, a twin-keeled Sadler 29, has had no difficulty on passages between Cornwall and Ireland or researching this book. Her statistics are:

LOA 8.67m
Beam 2.90m
Draught 1.12m
Displacement 3,839kg
Ballast 1,649kg
Engine 20HP Bukh
Crew 1 or 2
Fuel with reserves 128 litre
Water plus reserves 170 litre
(Stowage of rubbish on a small boat is a problem; this is difficult to dispose of in many harbours.)

Berthing and anchoring

For cruising these coasts a boat must have good ground tackle with plenty of cable for anchoring. Visitor space in marinas is under pressure from local boat-owners and visitors'

moorings may all be taken. These are usually yellow and heavy with a single ring and display maximum weight of boat. They sometimes have a rope pick-up of doubtful provenance. Most are laid by the appropriate county council and are usually surveyed every two years; those laid by a harbour authority are serviced annually. Neither organisation has spare staff so it is rare to be charged for anchoring or mooring. A few harbours display mooring fees and where to pay them. Only harbours with frequent commercial traffic have a harbourmaster with authority. Other harbours may list one, but he is often known as the harbour constable; he will advise but has no power. In some cases details are given of a helpful boatman or pub.

Marinas are few and under-staffed. If there is no reply on VHF, or to a telephone call, go to an outside berth; you will soon be met. A few marinas do not accept payment by credit card. It is sometimes possible to raft up to a fishing vessel on a quay after a word with the skipper. They are usually very helpful.

There are many safe anchorages that are not shown in any pilot book or on the chart. Those that are will be fairly comfortable as well as safe. ('Pull' – usually known as scend – means it is not always possible to lie comfortably in a berth or anchorage.) Much theoretical nonsense is written about anchoring but skippers know the anchors which suit their boats. Provided there is swinging room, put out as much chain as possible; it is of no use in the locker. Small yachts which cannot stow much chain should add plenty of warp. Nylon plait is good as it absorbs shocks and stows well. For these waters a cruising boat should have at least two bower anchors as well as a kedge, each with its own cable. Never anchor from bow and stern in a strong tideway as the aft anchor is sure to drag at the turn of tide. If mooring with two anchors, set both from the bow on a swivel attached to a separate riser. Equal scopes, set for expected currents and wind, make it easy to centre the boat between anchors. This makes anchoring in a restricted space practicable, but inform other craft anchoring nearby where your anchors are.

Beware of anchoring a twin-keeler where she will completely dry in an estuary with strong tides. When the tide turns she may be pushed sideways before lifting with the cable fouling a keel. If you prefer to lie peacefully to your own anchor do not 'let go' near visitors' moorings. In high season some yachts queue for these and may foul your anchor in the scramble to get a mooring. The first you may know is when you drag!

The tender

A robust load-carrying tender, equipped with oars, anchor and long mooring ropes is needed for exploring from remote anchorages and for long victualling trips. It is advisable to carry a set of mini-flares, a good torch and a hand-held VHF. Visibility can fall suddenly so take a small compass. In the Republic it is compulsory for anyone aboard a boat with a LOA of 7m or less to wear a life-jacket, unless going swimming or the boat is moored. There are age restrictions for operating powered craft, and these rules are strictly enforced. Full details are available from the Department of Communications, Marine and Natural Resources. See www.dcmnr.gov.ie

Repairs and spares

'All facilities' in this guide excludes chandlery. Rope and tackle for fishing vessels is available in most ports. For good chandlery and repairs see *Appendix*.

WEATHER FORECASTS

Met Éireann issues a new sea area (30 miles off the coast) forecast every 6 hours from 2359 (LT), which is then broadcast by CGR and RTÉ Radio 1, together with coastal weather reports. CGR gives details of small craft warnings; Radio 1 just mentions them. A warning indicates that Gale Force 6 or more is expected up to 10 miles offshore. Warnings are only issued in the recognised sailing season. Forecasts are given, clockwise, from significant headlands around Ireland. (These are listed in this guide and in the almanac.) There is no political demarcation – the coastal counties of Northern Ireland are included. (Northern Ireland comprises six of the nine counties of the Province of Ulster.) Sea area forecasts are for a 24-hour period with a further 24-hour outlook. CGR, after a call on Ch 16, broadcasts these on working channel every 3 hours from 0103 local time. Actual station reports are always given. CGR also gives reports from five QY(5)6s met-buoys: M1 is about 60 miles off Galway Bay, M2 between Anglesey and Dublin, M3 about 50 miles SW of Mizen Head and M4 north of Belmullet. M5 is SW of Carnsore Point. (Co-ordinates of these are sometime given by CGR.) CGR concludes reports, when necessary, with sea states for ferry crossings between Ireland, the UK and France. Valentia CGR also transmits Navtex information and broadcasts UK shipping forecasts for Shannon and Fastnet on MF 1752kHz at 0833 and 2033 UTC and on request. Domestic 'Weatherdial' for all sea areas is 1550 123850 and for Munster (South West Ireland) it is 1550 123855. This is not expensive and has no preliminary advertisements.

Radio 1 repeats the Sea Area Forecast and actuals daily at 0602, 1253, 1655 and 2355 (LT) plus general forecasts, with five-day outlook at 0755, 1255 and 1755. So the 0602 is almost up to the minute! Radio 1 can be received from western UK and off southern Ireland on 567kHz (MW) and 252kHz (LW). Around Ireland high power FM transmitters are best. Listen on 95.2 (NE), 89.1 (E), 89.6 (SE), 90.0 (SW), 88.8 (W) and 88.2 (NW). Some areas have a dedicated frequency which is given in the appendix. For all frequencies, and details of Irish and British Radio and TV programmes, get the weekly RTÉ Guide. The times of Radio 1's sea area and general forecasts can change. The Irish Times prints a good synoptic chart, with area forecasts, a five-day outlook and tide times. The Irish Independent gives similar information without the tides. BBC Radio Cornwall 630kHz (MW) and BBC Radio Devon 801kHz (MW) can be received in most of Cork and Kerry. Professional forecasters give a general forecast with five-day outlook during the main morning, mid-day and late afternoon news programmes, together with the current coastal conditions. These forecasts are a very good guide to the probable weather in Cork and Kerry. Radio Cornwall and Radio Devon also repeat relevant parts of the UK Shipping Forecast. Times of these broadcasts change. There are also independent commercial radio stations throughout Cork and Kerry which give weather forecasts.

Radio Listeners' Guide gives the frequencies, with much else, of all radio broadcast stations in the British Isles (which includes the Republic). Published annually by Clive Woodyear, PO Box 88, Plymouth, PL8 1YJ ☎ 0752 872888 *Email* enquiries@radiolistenersguide.co.uk www.radiolistenersguide.co.uk

Tides

The Standard Port for tides in this guide is Cóbh (Cork):

MHWS	MHWN	MLWS	MLWN
4.1m	3.2m	0.4m	1.3m

Tides get progressively a little later with slightly less range proceeding west and north from Cóbh and conversely east of Cóbh. Predictions for Cóbh are adequate for most purposes and the HW time given for each port is the average difference from HW Cóbh. The only tidal stream atlas for the area is Michael Reeve-Fowkes' *Tidal Atlas for the Western Channel* published by Adlard Coles

Nautical and sold online by Imray. *Western Channel* covers southern Ireland and Saint George's Channel, the Bristol Channel, the English Channel to Poole and Cherbourg then south to Brest. It shows the numerous eddies, especially in the bays – which were made by scouring contra-flows in the first place. Streams for harbour approaches are shown in relation to local HW and these are based on information given in ICP (see page 8).

HAZARDS

Lights and natural hazards

There are few coastal lights; these are mainly for fishing vessels, local sailors and coasters whose masters have route experience. Some harbours are rock-bound natural inlets which are dangerous for a stranger to enter at night. Reefs which barely cover abound to trap the unwary. Seemingly sandy bays are scattered with large boulders – erratics – dropped by glaciers. One side of such a bay may be completely foul. These are not places to sound into without local knowledge so add at least a metre, mentally, to your draught.

Early morning mists can drift over an anchorage, especially from inland lagoons, with the land breeze of night. There can be down-draughts from 'sheltering' high ground. Under a cliff these will be close in; from a smooth mountain gusts will be further out.

Salmon nets

From 1st June to 31st July legal attended salmon drift-nets are set Monday to Thursday from 0400 to 2100. Illegal and unguarded nets may be set until September. Atlantic salmon always return to the river where they were spawned, using smell to navigate and tides to assist their passage. They bunch up around headlands which is where the nets, a mile or so long, are usually laid. The salmon will be mainly homing in around peninsulas to the west of their native river. Nets have very small floats between conspicuous (sometimes!) inner and outer markers. If there is any type of boat, stationary or slowly patrolling off the coast, go well outside it. There is no point in planning the shortest route to the next headland in June and July. If a net is not spotted the nets-men will race over, gesticulating and shouting! Promptly going about will bring smiles all round. (The nets-men may also call you on VHF Ch 6 or 16.) In poor visibility keep at least three miles off. Nets are also set inside harbours that have a sizeable river. Most rivers from Waterford to the Shannon have a run of salmon and sea trout.

Fishing vessel guarding typical salmon net

This type of net is encountered often

Marine farms

Fish farms are numerous, mainly for mussels, especially in large natural harbours. Mussel farms have parallel rows of blue or grey barrels from which netting 'ropes' are suspended. The rows are far enough apart for a large harvesting vessel, with a crane, to work between – often at night with strong head-lamps.

Do not go between the rows of barrels. There is always a way through, about a cable wide, but in these pots may be laid! (Major marine farms are shown in ISDs and on corrected charts.) They do not encroach on recognised anchorages – yet – though their vessels are monopolising many quays. So it is important for pleasure craft to continue using these anchorages in order to keep them open. Salmon farms have floating cages but do not take up so much space. Farms should have lit yellow buoys, but smaller ones may be neither marked nor lit – another reason for not sailing at night.

Harvesting mussels in bay by Glengarriff Castle

IRISH COASTGUARD (IRCG), COMMUNICATIONS AND SAFETY

Coastguard Radio (CGR) is manned by professional radio officers. They co-ordinate all maritime safety, search and rescue services in the Republic, calling upon shore and water-based coastguards, the RNLI (which has lifeboats in strategic ports) and Irish SAR helicopters. In 2004 independent inshore boats were being introduced for rescue and inshore safety patrol. CGR is always called on a working channel. Emergencies are worked on 16, 67 and working channel; there is no 'channel zero' as in UK. The Republic

has only three manned Coast Guard Radio Stations. These are:

Dublin Maritime Rescue Co-ordination Centre (MRCC) VHF Ch 83, with relay aerials at Carlingford (04), Wicklow Head (02), Rosslare (23) and Mine Head (83).

Valentia Maritime Rescue Sub-Centre (MRSC) VHF Ch 24 & MF 1752kHz, with relay stations at Cork (26), Mizen (04), Bantry Bay (23), Shannon (28) and Galway (04).

Malin Head MRSC VHF Ch 23 & MW 1677MHz, with relay stations at Clifden (26), Belmullet (83), Donegal Bay (02) and Glen Head (24).

The UK's Belfast Coastguard (MRSC) VHF Ch 16, liaises closely with IRCG.

Ship-shore link calls are available, so if you expect one it is necessary to pass a track report (TR) for your vessel to be included in the appropriate traffic list. These are broadcast after navigation warnings at every odd H+33 (LT) except 0133 and 0533. These warnings are important; quite often they are for lights and marks of significance only to fishing vessels and small craft. Communication through the nearest CGR aerial is not always possibly because of terrain, so try the adjacent station: a call on Ch 67 usually gets a reply. Excessive reporting of movements is not encouraged but CGR likes to be kept informed of the area where a yacht is cruising. Keep in touch with a shore contact who has the telephone number of, say, Valentia MRSC (☎ +353 66 9476109 from abroad).

A domestic radio with MW, FM and LW bands, together with a marine VHF, is sufficient. The south and west seaboard of the Republic had only an MF DSC Service until 2005. Now there is a VHF DSC service but it is advisable to make distress calls on Ch 16 as well. For general communications a mobile/cellphone with an Irish SIM card is very useful. Calls from an Irish number are then national, not through your home country. This also makes on-board internet much cheaper. Most port towns now have an internet café. Vodafone (www.vodafone.ie) gives good coverage around the coasts and has an office in Cork and sub-offices in some towns. O² (www.shop.o2.ie) is the other major provider in Ireland. It is handy to keep a second mobile roaming on a SIM card bought in your own country.

Telephone

When dialling from outside Ireland the IDD code is +353. Note that most telephone numbers in this guide are given without IDD.

Malin Head MRSC
1677 kHz
VHF Ch 23

Fair Hd

55°N

Bloody Foreland

Glen Head
VHF 24 • Rossan Pt

THE NORTH

Belfast Lough

BELFAST •

Donegal Bay
VHF 02

Erris Hd

Belmullet
VHF 83

Belfast MRSC (UK)
VHF Ch 16

54°

CONNAUGHT

Carlingford
VHF 04 • *Carlingford Lough*

IRELAND

Irish Sea

Clifden
VHF 26

Dublin MRCC
VHF Ch 83

• *Howth Hd*

Slyne Hd

Galway
VHF 04

53°

LEINSTER

Wicklow Head
VHF 02

Loop Head

Shannon
VHF 28

Rosslare
VHF 23

Valentia MRSC
1752 kHz
VHF Ch 24

MUNSTER

• *Carnsore Pt*
Hook Hd

52°

Cork
VHF 26

Mine Head
VHF 83

Roche's Point

Bantry
VHF 23

Mizen Head

Mizen
VHF 04

51°

11°   10°W   9°   8°   7°   6°   5°

PILOTAGE AND NAVIGATION

A reliable autohelm is very helpful. The skipper may have several crew but he or she may be single-handed – if the pilotage is tricky!

Good 7 x 50 binoculars, preferably with a built-in magnetic (not flux-gate) compass, are a most important aid. Similarly, a bearing compass with a swinging needle is the only type for pilotage.

The Mark 1 eyeball is the best aid for coasting Cork and Kerry, backed by information from an area navaid such as GPS, used in navigational mode. Bear in mind that many of the anchorages and old harbours, including offshore rocks, have not been surveyed since the 19th century (refer to *Source Data* on each chart), so do not plot a GPS waypoint close to the shore. Co-ordinates on OSI maps differ very slightly from those on nautical charts; where a co-ordinate is given it refers to a hard bit on the chart. Do not use it for GPS navigation! The suitability of any anchorage is at the discretion of the reader. This guide is mainly for day sailing in good visibility but radar is good to have as mist and fog can form when least expected.

DGPS stations give a very accurate bearing using an MF direction finder. There is no call-sign; identification is by expected bearing. All DGPS stations in the British Isles and coastal Europe from Denmark to Spain are listed in the almanac.

Charts, pilots and nautical publications
See *Appendix*

Magnetic variation
It is important to know this within a degree, as much of the visual pilotage has to be by bearings and transits. The method to display variations has, to date, led to considerable errors even on corrected charts. The UK Hydrographic Office say that they are reviewing the method of determining current variation on new charts, as the present method of extrapolation is not accurate over time. If in doubt, consult the variation on OSI Discovery Series maps, which are republished more frequently than Admiralty Charts.

Chart symbols
It is important to know the symbols used for dangerous rocks, wrecks, lanbys and other large floating marks. These are given on the back of Imray C charts and in *AC 5011* – a booklet of all symbols and abbreviations used on Admiralty and Imray charts.

Fastnet Rock

Lights
Lights, Light Vessels, Lanbys and Racons for each cruising area are listed and described in the current almanac and in the Admiralty *List of Lights Vol A (NP 74)*.

The Port of Cork – safe harbour for ships

Plans of harbours and anchorages
Descriptions of topographical and man-made marks and hazards supplement the entry directions on charts and plans where applicable. Characteristics of important pilotage lights and marks are only shown on the plans. These should always be checked against a corrected current almanac. All bearings are relative to true north, and towards the feature unless otherwise stated. Where necessary photographs state the direction from which taken. For many anchorages the plan will be the only diagram available, but most have a photograph. Where a position in the text is 'as shown by GPS' this is corrected to WGS 84 Datum.

Abbreviations used in the text

ISDs – Irish Cruising Club *Sailing Directions: South and West Coasts of Ireland*

ICP – *Irish Coast Pilot* (Admiralty Sailing Directions)

almanac – *Reed's Almanac* or *Reed's Western Almanac*, or *The Cruising Almanac* or almanac of your choice

OSI – Ordnance Survey of Ireland Discovery Series 2cm:1km maps

AC – Admiralty chart

C – Imray chart

FACILITIES AND SHOPPING

Electricity, water, gas and diesel

In marinas, which are seldom as sophisticated but never as expensive as elsewhere in Europe, AC (electricity) is free or metered fairly. Taps in harbours often require a push-on adapter. Camping Gaz (Gaz) and Calor Butane (Calor) are usually available in harbours and towns. Calor Propane has to be refilled in Cork. Calor Kosangas (Kos) is always available; if several cruises are planned it is worth buying cylinders and a regulator. Extension AC leads and extra water-hose may be needed. Some states in Europe provide diesel fuel for marine use at a reduced rate of tax. This has a distinctive colour. In the UK it is known as 'red diesel', but in the Republic of Ireland it is coloured green.

Butcher in Crosshaven

Shopping

Shops, including supermarkets, seldom open before 0900. Credit cards are accepted in all but the smallest shop, and there are ATMs (cash dispensers) in many stores – large or small. Cheques drawn in the currency of a foreign bank will be accepted sometimes – if a credit card is not. Laundrettes are not often self-service. Take washing in early and it will be ready for collection by late afternoon.

Victuals

Keeping provisions fresh can be a problem; fridges are expensive on energy and many have limited capacity. A large built-in and well-drained ice-box is very efficient. Even in the warmest weather *Balair* has a cold box which only needs a weekly injection of ice. Most pubs will gladly supply this, as will the fish departments of supermarkets – with no payment asked. A euro in the pub's lifeboat or store's charity box is appreciated. Never offer a tip; it will not be accepted. This also applies for trawler ice, though the shoveller will appreciate a can in your bucket. Fish ice keeps longer than drinking ice, which is usually available in supermarkets.

The major supermarket is SuperValu, though others from the rest of Europe may be found. All have really excellent fresh meats, fish and take-away cold and hot foods. Vegetables (particularly potatoes) are sold for their taste, not to look appealing.

Small tins of vegetables and fruit are difficult to find, as are good biscuits to go with cheese. An excellent snack with afternoon tea is brack – a pleasantly spiced fruit loaf which keeps fresh forever! Though pork is the favoured meat, pork pies do not exist. The provenance of all meat and poultry is displayed; 99% is raised in Ireland. If a supermarket has no coffee-shop there will always be a nearby café for breakfast. Most petrol service-stations have a fresh food counter, so if out for the day there is no need to make a picnic.

Alcohol

Good wines are available in most food stores, but beers and spirits are found only in big supermarkets or the rare off-licence. Pubs will sell these over the counter. Scotch whisky is expensive in supermarkets but there is usually one brand of proprietary Scotch at a discount. Irish whiskey is expensive but very good; ask for Paddy, Bushmills or Jamesons (with a short 'a'). The stouts of Cork are Beamish and Murphy's, though Liffey Water is always available and is preferred in Kerry. Whether your tipple is stout, wine, paddy or gin, the toast it *sláinte* ('slan-tchuh').

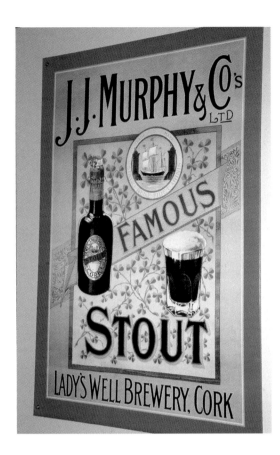

Pubs and eating out

Pubs are good value at lunch-time and there is no need to order any sort of drink. In the evenings they are more for the young; the *céilí* ('kay-lee') – music, singing and sometimes dancing – and the *craic* ('crack') – general conviviality – are noisy! Take a harmonica and you will be warmly welcomed. Evening food is usually only available in an expensive dining room. This is when the seniors might eat and relax aboard, though part of the enjoyment of cruising is discovering pubs and restaurants to suit taste and pocket. Traditional Irish dishes may be difficult to find ashore. Hotels serving a lunch-time carvery give excellent value.

On-board entertainment

Excellent programmes on RTÉ Radio 1 include *Sunday Miscellany* at 0910 (FM only) and *Seascapes* at 1930 on Thursday, repeated at 0530 on Saturday. This is 'The Maritime Programme for this Island Nation' and is presented by RTÉ's Marine Correspondent, Tom MacSweeney, together with a very evocative rendering of *Sailing By*. He sails his yacht *Seascapes* out of Cork. RTÉ's Lyric FM, on 99.6 FM throughout the area, broadcasts light and classical music, with little chat and few advertisements. Do not worry if a programme is late; RTÉ has an endearing habit of over-running programmes rather than cutting short an interview or good argument!

Voices and Poetry of Ireland is an anthology compiled by Brian Molloy and published by HarperCollins (2003). The words of each piece come alive when heard on the CDs – which come with this lovely book – recorded by poets, actors, radio presenters and other personalities..

For a local paper get *The Cork Examiner* or *The Kerryman*.

A familiar sight around the Dingle peninsula – the curragh is still much in use
Cork Kerry Tourism

Footpath way mark

THE ENVIRONMENT

Nearly all domestic refuse is recycled but it is always difficult to dispose of galley waste. Even in fishing ports skips are chained to accept only small amounts. Litter bins have very small openings and it is illegal to put rubbish in them, so keep bottles for the bigger ports with bottle ('bring') banks. Stores do not give plastic shopping bags. These cost 15c each (but you will be given paper bags on request). It is difficult to find small refuse bags. Press-zip bags are also hard to come by, but delicious sliced stone-ground bread comes in reusable ones.

There are no public footpaths but a few paths are signposted Public Right of Way. Until recently, access to private land was not restricted. Now many tracks display notices to the effect that those entering do so at their own risk – or worse!

HEALTH

Residents of the EU get free consultation and treatment by doctors and dentists; any medicines prescribed will be free regardless of age. A completed E111 (new format available from UK post offices and in the EU) and photographic ID are necessary. Only tender a photocopy of the E111. There is no appointment for an initial consultation; it is 'first come first treated'. Limited hospital treatment is free for citizens of the EU but it is wise to have appropriate health and travel insurance.

All major landing places display notices prohibiting the import of fresh meat and dairy produce; eat or dispose of imported food as instructed.

Smoking

The Republic strictly enforces a 'No Smoking' law in public places. For the non-smoker this is excellent, but this blanket rule does not take smokers into account. It has opened up more beer gardens, but now fewer colourful characters sit outside a bar supping stout; instead this seating is usually occupied by smokers.

RELIGION

The main religions in Ireland are Roman Catholic (RC) and Church of Ireland (C of I) (Protestant). The Catholic Angelus is rung at 1200 and 1800. For most it is just a time signal, but it is polite to be silent if others are.

ACTIVITIES ASHORE

Golf, tennis and horse-riding are nearly always available in or near port towns. Appropriate attire is required for these. Fly fishing for trout is free – no licence or permission is required for stream fishing. Anglers can be as scruffy as they like (but see notes about access to private land under *The Environment*). Angling for salmon or seatrout does require a licence. Cruising sailors are well placed to observe resident, migratory and overwintering birds. Botanists can search for rare native plants on the islands. (Monasteries and castles sometimes have rare plants imported by Crusaders and other ancients.) Serious cycling and walking routes are published. Mountaineering is only for the experienced. Take suitable precautions before lone walks.

The GAA

The GAA (Gaelic Athletic Association) was founded in 1885 when the Irish no longer wished to play English games. Principal sports are Gaelic football and hurling. The football, played with a round ball, has features of rugby and association football and some from netball. Hurling looks like a very skilful mix of hockey and rugby, except that the ball is carried on a hurley! Both games score under or over the bar. Each team has its own 'ensign', worn by a supporter's house and car.

DRIVING AND TRANSPORT

Driving is on the left, using the same highway code as in Britain. Irish drivers are extremely courteous and they usually give way to pedestrians. Seat belts are compulsory. The speed limit on motorways and dual carriage is 112kmph (70mph), otherwise it is 96kmph (60mph). Speed signs were still in mph in 2004 but were due to go metric in 2005. Old black-on-white finger-posts give distances in miles; the new green signs in kilometres. It is customary for slow vehicles to use the hard shoulder to assist overtaking traffic. (National Primary Roads have a hard shoulder of consistent width. Do not park on this.) All designated picnic and parking places on main roads have a height restriction, but car parks at scenic places usually have unrestricted headroom. A good motoring and tourist road map for all of Ireland is Michelin *712 Ireland*, 1cm:4km. *Holiday Map South*, 4cm:10km covers all of Cork and Kerry. (Appropriate OSI and Michelin maps are usually available locally.)

Distances by road

From Cork	km
Youghal	48
Kinsale	30
Baltimore	94
Crookhaven	120
Bantry	94
Kenmare	98
Castletownbere	146
Cahersiveen	145
Dingle	170
Tralee	120
Shannon to Kilrush	70
Rosslare to Cork	add 193
From Cork Ro-Ro Ferry	add 18

Cork Airport is halfway, time-wise, between the city and Kinsale. Kerry Faranfore Airport is 20 minutes from Tralee and has international connections.

Self-drive car hire

See *Appendix*

USEFUL PHRASES

Hello *dia dhuit* (pronounced 'dee a gwit')
Welcome *fáilte* ('fawl-chah')
Please *le do hoil* ('ledda huil')
Thank you *go raibh maith agat* ('gurrah maha gut')
Goodbye *slàn* ('slan')
Cheers *sláinte* ('slan-tchuh')
Men's toilet *Fir*
Women's toilet *Mná*
Police *Gardai* ('gardee')
The Irish Parliament is the *Dáil* ('doyle') *Éireann*
The Prime Minister is the *Taoiseach* ('toshack')
A Member of the Irish Parliament is a TD *Teachta* (Deputy) *Dáil*
Incomers are known as 'blow-ins'.

Do not forget to roll your 'r's or pronounce them as 'or' at the start of a word as in RTÉ ('Or-tay-ee'). Pronounce *'ea'* as in 'fate' and *'gh'* as 'her'. For *currach* say 'curruck' and if you want (illegal) *poteen* ask for 'putcheen'. A phrase book (with pronunciation) is handy.

RECIPES

My wife Joy has included some of our favourite local Irish recipes. She writes, 'All Irish cooking is adaptable: the recipes having been handed down from generation to generation. Many traditional Irish cooks still produce delectable meals with the standard recipes but on a boat this is sometimes difficult. The Irish are very keen on their cooking and will be happy to discuss it with you; you might even be offered a treasured family recipe. Take advice from the butcher as to cuts of meat and cooking methods for your chosen meal; they always welcome strangers who want to learn the secrets of their country's cuisine.

Bread has been suggested as a good accompaniment to most meals. We all know about Irish soda bread, but there are others, too. Thanks to Odlum's we can quickly produce tasty, freshly baked bread of many varieties. These small bags of bread mix are available from most SuperValu supermarkets and some other shops. They range from the usual soda bread, through farmhouse brown, hearty cracked wheat, honey and sunflower seed and many more. Preparation and cooking instructions are simple – no kneading needed! – and in 40–45 minutes you have a hot, crusty 2lb loaf. If you haven't got a 2lb bread tin, used a 6-inch square oven tin. Line this with greased foil, filling in the corners to give at least the appearance of a round tin, and you will be proud of your typical Irish loaf. Serve your work of art with the delicious butter of which Ireland is justifiably proud and you will receive fitting compliments on your culinary skills.

In this land of the potato, even the most traditional of Irish cooks will add to their dishes vegetables which are not strictly of historic veracity, so you can use up all those potatoes, carrots, parsnips, etc. which remain in your vegetable locker without spoiling the original recipe. Leeks in Ireland are succulent and tasty so, more often than not, we use these instead of onions. (The only advantage to onions is that they stay fresh longer should you be offshore for long periods.)

Stuck in harbour, as was *Balair* for many weeks in 2004, what could be more fun than spending a few hours experimenting with cooking new and exciting boat meals? Small, inexpensive recipe books abound. *Bon appetit*.

RECOMMENDED BOOKS

See *Appendix*

SEA BIRDS

Notes by Judith Pentreath and Des Lavelle

About thirty-five species of sea birds nest around the coasts of Ireland. Some are migratory, others native and some pelagic, i.e. they only leave the oceans to breed. In the nesting season the cruising sailor will see many of these, skimming the waves, flying by or in great rafts on the water. Their names may not be known so the illustrations will help in identifying some seen from the boat.

Two species are fantastic aviators, as they skim the waves in search of food for their brood. The pelagic Manx shearwater spends the winter mainly off the coasts of Brazil and Argentina. It returns to breed in early summer. White underneath, black on top, its rapid wing-beats are followed by seemingly endless skimming of the waves on down-swept wings. Very prone to predation by large gulls, it only visits its nesting burrow in the turf after dark, with an exchange of noisy guidance signals. When not flying it forms some of the largest rafts as it awaits dusk and feeding time.

The other great glider is the fulmar, with a similar flight to, but larger than, the shearwater. This bird likes to circle ships. It nests and lives year-round on coastal cliffs. The delicate and tiny British storm petrel is unmistakable. It is black with a white rump and flutters and flits around the boat. Like the seven other petrels it is pelagic and overwinters off South Africa.

The kittiwake is a small pelagic gull with inky wing-tips. In fresh winds it effortlessly rides the up-draughts over the waves; when protecting its cliff-edge nests it is very raucous.

An amusing bird is the guillemot. In flight it shows a lot of white on its undersides, but sitting low on the water is appears dark and quite small. All summer just one parent bird gives its fledglings diving lessons. Sometimes they will swim out of the way, but usually they quizzically hesitate before diving just in time! The guillemot nests in large cliff-side colonies before returning to a life on the ocean.

The razorbill is related to the guillemot but is less prolific and has a larger neck and distinctive bill. These tend to whiz away from the boat at high speed. On the shore line it spends much time seeing off other feeding birds!

A common shoreline scavenger (not illustrated) is the hooded crow, easily identified by its grey cowl. It is common in the northwestern British Isles and in eastern Europe.

The great skua would be a rare sighting as it breeds in the Scottish islands and only visits Irish waters in spring and autumn. It is short-tailed and broad winged compared with the other skuas. It prefers the pickings of other bird to fishing for itself and will also take smaller birds and their eggs. A pelagic species, it will be seen mainly in flight and spends most of its life at sea. Finally, we all know the quaint puffin, with its colourful breeding-season bill full of sand eels, fluttering over and through the wave-tops. It nests in the same way as the shearwater and is pelagic in the winter. Viewing these birds at sea, you have a great advantage over most ornithologists. But do not disturb a raft of birds. Should you be fortunate to be anchored at dusk in a creek, with shearwaters, guillemots, razorbills and puffins, bringing in 'all-day breakfasts' for their broods (albeit late for the young shearwaters) criss-crossing overhead, you may marvel why they never have mid-air collisions.

Illustrations by Lucy Wilson

Guillemot in flight

Razorbill in flight

Puffin in flight

Razorbill on water with unfledged young

Guillemot on water with unfledged young

Manx Shearwater
skimming waves

Razorbill standing on
water's edge

Fulmar in flight

Storm Petrel

Storm Petrel in flight

Kittiwake standing

Kittiwake (juvenile) on
water

Fulmar

Great Skua in flight

Storm Petrel on water

Manx Shearwater on
water

1 YOUGHAL TO KINSALE

Crosshaven. Towards the
harbour entrance, Roche's
Point and Power Head

1 YOUGHAL TO KINSALE

Ports, harbours and anchorages
Youghal – Ballycotton – Cork
Ringabella Bay – Roberts Cove –
Oyster Haven – Kinsale

Arrival ports
Cork (Crosshaven) or Kinsale

Charts and maps
Passage and planning charts
Imray C57, AC 2049
Additional browsing charts
AC 2740, 1765
OSI Discovery Series maps 77, 76,
82, 81, 87

**Coastguard radio relay stations
with working channels**
Rosslare Ch 23
Mine Head Ch 83
Cork Ch 26
Mizen Head Ch 04

RNLI Lifeboats
Youghal, Ballycotton, Crosshaven,
Kinsale

Important landfall lights
Conningbeg
Hook Head
Mine Head
Ballycotton
Roche's Point

Tourist Information:
Cork Kerry Tourism, Aras Fáilte,
Grand Parade, Cork
☎ 021 4273251 *Fax* 021 4273504
Email info@corkkerrytourism.ie
www.ireland.travel.ie

A BRIEF DESCRIPTION OF THE AREA

Arriving from the Irish Sea, from Wales and the south west, Cork is an ideal initial destination. One of the world's great harbours, it can be entered safely in any weather, any tide and at night. Well-sheltered Crosshaven, with three marinas, is just inside the entrance with an easy and well-lit approach. Should the weather become unsuitable for coastal cruising, a week could well be spent visiting Cork, historic Cóbh, East Passage with its lovely marina and on to the Belvelly Channel north of Great Island, commonly known as 'behind the island'. This has a very sheltered and attractive anchorage from which interesting explorations can be made by tender; even back to the marina for stout and a meal. East Ferry Marina is very popular with local sailors and adventurous visitors. Modern yachts are available for bare-boat charter in Cork and Kinsale, crews

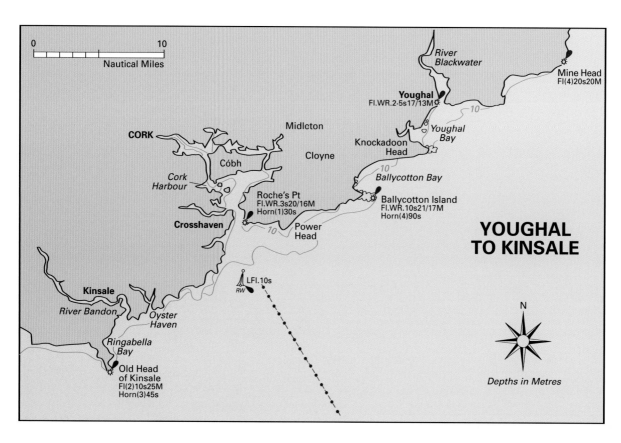

being collected from Cork's air or ferry port (see *Appendix*).

Kinsale, 15 miles west of Cork, would be the better choice for an initial arrival if you are keen to be heading west. It is easy to enter by day or night, at any tide, except if there is a very strong south-easterly wind. It has a mix of commercial and pleasure craft, two marinas a possible alongside pontoon berth and a few visitors moorings. Kinsale Yacht Club's excellent marina should be your first choice. You will receive a warm welcome at your berth and in the lovely clubhouse. The historic town is to hand, famous for its restaurants, but over-crowded with tourists in high summer. Cork and Kinsale are fully described below as we coast from the east with *Balair*. For the single or short-handed crew routeing from Britain via Milford Haven, Kilmore Quay Marina makes a very attractive stopover, with good shopping and pubs.

Should Kilmore Quay figure in your cruise plan it is reassuring to have AC 2740 (1:25,000) for the Saltee Islands and St Patrick's Bridge – the shallow spit which joins those islands to Kilmore Quay. The lateral buoys for St Patrick's Bridge are laid for eastbound traffic. (This applies to offshore marks round Cork and Kerry.) Kilmore and Dungarvan (drying pontoon or anchor in pool) are very attractive, with all facilities. Kilmore can get very crowded with boats 'rafted in', but there is a comfortable passage anchorage east of Forlorn Point. An alternative anchorage is off Great Saltee's landing place. Outside Dungarvan, Helvick has visitors' buoys and anchorage well-sheltered from the southwest.

KILMORE QUAY TO YOUGHAL

Until west of Waterford the land is low-lying with long beaches (hereafter 'strands') and coastal loughs. Hook Head lighthouse is impressive, its base an ancient 24-metre high white tower with a 22-metre lighthouse atop. 10 miles to the west, on Great Newton Head, are three tall towers. On one stands a 'Metal Man' pointing out to sea, indicating that this is not the entrance to Waterford. Watch for many pots if closing to view these interesting marks. From Hook Head, the next headland of note is Mine Head, with a lighthouse. The Rogue dries just to the east. The agricultural hinterland, with dairy herds and cultivated fields becomes more wild approaching Ram Head, which has a conspicuous square tower. Nearing Youghal, huge chunks of limestone and sandstone have dropped vertically to form roofless cavities. Cliffs continue thus to Whiting Bay, just before the entrance to Youghal, with bracken-covered tops sloping steeply seaward.

YOUGHAL

This is the easternmost harbour of County Cork. East Cork was initially settled by Anglo-Norman invaders in the late 12th century. At the mouth of the River Blackwater, Youghal ('Yawl') is still used by shallow-draught coasters which can cross the bar. There are rocks and a ledge in the bay, both marked by lit cardinal buoys, in the red sector of Youghal lighthouse – the only approach aid. For a yacht a fair weather entry is easy, at any tide. A night approach is best left to the occasional freighter, fishing vessels

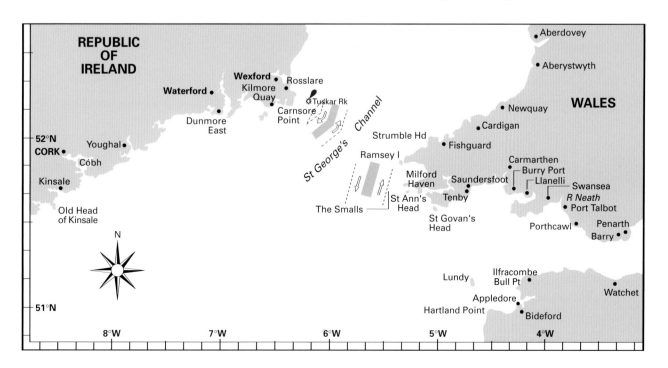

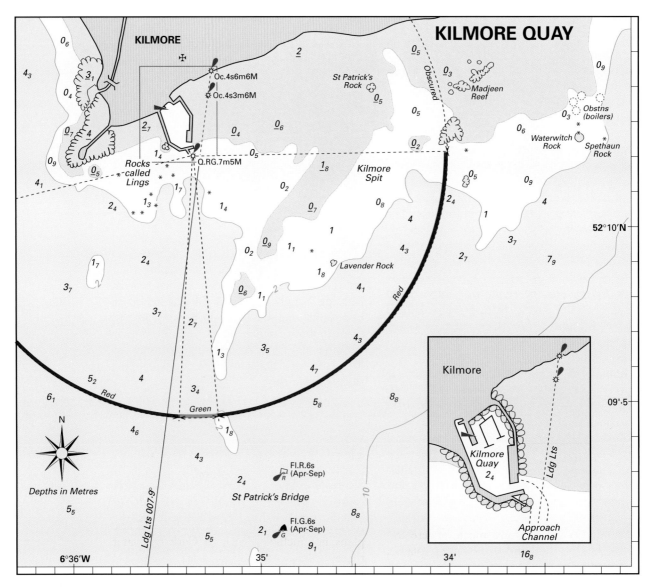

KILMORE

KILMORE QUAY

Oc.4s6m6M
Oc.4s3m6M
Q.RG.7m5M

Rocks called Lings

St Patrick's Rock

Obscured

Madjeen Reef

Obstns (boilers)

Waterwitch Rock

Spethaun Rock

Kilmore Spit

52°10'N

Lavender Rock

Red

Red

09'·5

Kilmore

Green

N

Depths in Metres

Kilmore Quay

Ldg Lts

Approach Channel

Ldg Lts 007.9°

Fl.R.6s (Apr-Sep) R

St Patrick's Bridge

Fl.G.6s (Apr-Sep) G

6°36'W

35'

34'

Hook Head

and others with local knowledge. In strong southerly winds the approach is dangerous.

An initial alongside berth is unlikely, nor are there visitors' moorings. There is no harbourmaster but Youghal Shipping may have a berth. Contact them for this and all other harbour information on VHF Ch 16/14 (HW±0300) or ☎ 024 92577. Several anchorages have good holding in mud and gravel, but are uncomfortable in fresh southerlies. There are no special facilities for yachtsmen and there is no yacht club but Ferry Point Boatyard (☎ 024 94232) is helpful. This once-fortified port has changed little since Sir Walter Raleigh was given huge estates here by his Queen, as was his friend Edmund Spenser who wrote many volumes of *The Faerie Queen* at nearby Kilcolman Castle. The castle was later burnt by rebels, Spenser and his family narrowly escaping with their lives. (Both these gentlemen were hated by the Irish.) There is good shopping, with golf, tennis, swimming and wet-land ornithology locally, as well as horse riding and fishing for trout and salmon.

Balair found very good holding in 4m about 2 cables NE of Ferry Point with the water tower bearing 260°. In fresh southerly winds it was too rough to go ashore safely by tender. This anchorage is only a short distance from the best all-tide landing place – by the car park just south of a pier, on piles, with a rickety landing stage. This pier has a tap but yachts can only berth at HW. Beware of long mooring ropes. Small 18th- and 19th-century docks dry to sand but small craft and fishing vessels make it impossible to berth, though these docks well suited the filming of *Moby Dick*.

Youghal's excellent Chamber of Tourism, in Market Square, Youghal, County Cork (☎ 024 92592 *Fax* 024 92502 www.youghalchamber.ie) is in the 19th-century Market House by the car park. It is worth getting *Youghal – Historic Walled Port* and the *Mini Guide to East Cork,* which, with the *East Cork Area Guide,* give the gardens, flora and fauna, ancient sites, farmers' markets, angling and much else accessible from the harbours of East Cork. By the lighthouse there is swimming and diving at HW, but currents can be strong, with a Blue Flag strand further on.

A street market is held on Saturdays near the SuperValu. There is also a Tesco supermarket. The Nook in Church Street, run by the same family since 1901, is a nice pub but does not do evening meals. There are many noisier pubs and good eating places. The Walter Raleigh Hotel serves a lunch-time carvery and inexpensive evening meals.

Cromwell's Arch, Youghal. He is said to have finally departed from Ireland through this arch in the medieval walls of this once fortified port

Motor cruisers and tenders can proceed many miles up the River Blackwater. Boatman Richie Power of Green River Marine runs canoe trips up the river and gives harbour advice. (The Chamber of Tourism has his details.) Before the upstream bridge (6.5m clearance at MHWS) was built, schooners and lighters traded upstream as far as Cappoquin. There is a pub and HW quay at Villerstown (OSI 81). Should your cruise plans not include a visit to Cork by water there is a frequent bus service to the Republic's second city.

Youghal from E

Chamber of Tourism

HW landing stage with water tap

Moby Dick pub

Best landing

Green Quay – Youghal Shipping

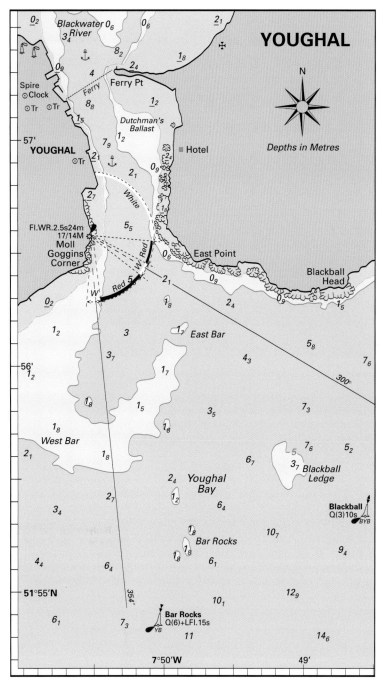

approaches can be dangerous. From the east it is difficult to pick out the entrance. From the southwest the entrance to the Blackwater River is conspicuous; it frames inland mountains.

The only close hazard when in the eastern white sector of Youghal LH, on the mean track of 300°, is the shore to starboard. Blackball Ledge (least depth 3.7m), mainly of concern to bigger vessels, will be to port. At 2 cables from the lighthouse turn into the harbour to bring Ferry Point on to 354°. Follow the deep (5–10m) channel midway between the heads then keep closer to the town shore, minded that this side shallows rapidly.

From the west, Bar Rocks will be just to starboard of the white sector (mean track 354°) of the lighthouse. Break off slightly to starboard 5 cables from the lighthouse and sound in as above. A night approach is not recommended for strangers as the lighthouse, soundings and the lights of the town are the only aids. The first anchorage is in deep water off the southern end of the town, about 5 cables inside the harbour. This has strong currents with a steeply shelving bank off the quays.

The bandstand mentioned in ISDs was black and white in 2003, with a pink and white holiday complex beyond. New drying banks northeast of Ferry Point are now incorporated in the charts. Youghal Shipping has concrete Green Quay, the most northerly on the front. This has 1.3m alongside with small patches which just dry off the quay. A fender board is needed for the tyres on the quay. Water is available, and diesel from a tanker on shipping days. Youghal gets about 40 visiting yachts a year and there is no large-scale commercial fishing industry, apart from salmon netting. The Blackwater is famous for its salmon.

YOUGHAL TO BALLYCOTTON

Continuing westward it is possible to sail between Knockadoon Head and Capel Island but this has reefs and strong streams. Capel Island has a white beacon – the base of an unfinished lighthouse. The head, with the island, is an important bird sanctuary and nets are laid south of the island.

The western half of Ballycotton Bay has a beautiful strand, curving past a marshy inlet to the small fishing harbour at Ballycotton. Ballycotton Island has an unusual black lighthouse. The powerful white sector, and that of Roche's Point at the entrance to Cork, make good landfall aids.

YOUGHAL PILOTAGE

Tides HW Cóbh+0005
Maximum stream over bars 1½kn at HW Cóbh +0320, average ¾kn
RLNI Inshore Lifeboat

Salmon nets are set south of Capel Island and in the relatively narrow neck between the town and Ferry Point. There is a netting station just below the new upstream road bridge.

When approaching listen on VHF 14 at HW±0300 for any shipping; there are 2–3 arrivals a week. The East Bar has a least charted depth of 2.8m and the West Bar 1.7m. The offshore rocks and ledge have lit cardinal buoys, both in the red sector of the lighthouse. In strong southerly winds the

BALLYCOTTON

There are visitors' moorings and an anchorage sheltered by Ballycotton and Small Islands. At low water there are small bathing beaches in and outside the harbour. Besides restaurants, hotels and a few pubs there is a nice store and post office. This is an important fishing port and select holiday resort. The harbour is crowded but very friendly. By arrangement an alongside overnight berth might be available on the east quay, which has water and ice. There is a small restaurant near the harbour. Spanish Point Guest House, owned by a fishing vessel skipper's wife, overlooks the anchorage and has an excellent restaurant. ☎ 021 4646177 *Email* spanishpoint@indigo.ie

Shanagarry, 1½ miles by tender (or anchor off the strand) is the home of Ireland's famous Ballymaloe Cookery School, offering courses and demonstrations. It has a large herb garden, shop and café. Quaker William Penn, who founded the American state of Pennsylvania, once lived near here. The filling station at Shanagarry has a small supermarket but the nearby caravan site cannot be recommended. It is possible to land at the northwest end of Ballycotton Island.

Ballytrasna, in the Gaeltacht (see *Introduction*) is reached by a cliff walk to the west of Ballycotton and has a sheltered sandy beach. 1km further west is a good example of

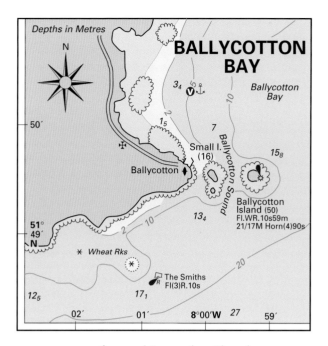

a promontory fort and in another 2km there is an old signal tower. Cloyne, 10km to the west, has a tall round-tower giving views over Cork harbour.

Ballycotton harbour from E

Looking E over
Ballycotton
Harbour to
Ballycotton Island
at HW

BALLYCOTTON PILOTAGE

Tides HW Cóbh –0005
Max stream in sound 2kn
RNLI All-weather Trent
Beware salmon drift nets set off Ballycotton Island

There is no large-scale chart so heed the advice in ISDs: 'The Smiths are a dangerous group of rocks which lie about 1.5M WSW of Ballycotton and are 0.5M offshore. They are marked by a R can light buoy Fl(3)R.10s moored SE of the shoal. Do not pass N of Wheat Rocks, which dry 1m and lie between the Smiths and the shore to the NW. Capel Island open S of Ballycotton Island clears all these dangers.' The sound is not recommended in southwest winds. It has a drying rock in the middle so keep closer to Ballycotton Island. Moorings and anchorages are to the north of the harbour. The full-time coxswain of the RNLI Trent all-weather lifeboat welcomes visitors to the boat-house. He will give advice on harbour facilities and onward pilotage.

BALLYCOTTON TO CORK HARBOUR (CROSSHAVEN)

Keep outside The Smiths rocks (lit PHM) then set course to either leave Pollock Rock (southeast of Power Head) to the north or take the inside passage. Capel Island, bearing 051° open southeast of Ballycotton Island clears all dangers, including Power SCM – 1 mile southeast of Pollock Rock. Cliffs are again high and rugged, with one long strand just east of Power Head. This has a disused fog-signal station and a radio mast. Gyleen, in Power Head Bay, has a pier and beach. It is much used by angling boats, hence Pollock Rock. Kinsale gas field, 28 miles sou'southwest of Roche's Point, is well lit but the pipeline comes ashore here so study the chart if anchoring. Cliffs now slope gently down to Roche's Point with its white cottages, lighthouse, towers, Anglo-Norman castle and a promontory fort. (Roche is a Norman name still used in East Cork.)

Cork's huge lower harbour (once known as Queenstown) can be entered on any tide, in any weather and at night. The entrance has west and east channels for shipping. Beware of the Cow and Calf Rocks close off Roche's Point. Cork Harbour Radio should be called on VHF Ch 12 or ☎ 021 4273125 with your intentions; they will advise on any commercial traffic. Two sets of leading marks, for the shipping channels, are on the east shore. A colourful fishing village, drying to a rocky foreshore, lies inside Roche's Point. Above Canavan Point, 'Roche's Point Automatic' weather station can be seen through binoculars. There are impressive 18th-century forts, Meagher to port and Davis to starboard, as the entrance opens into Cork Harbour. This is where great clippers awaited orders for their cargoes.

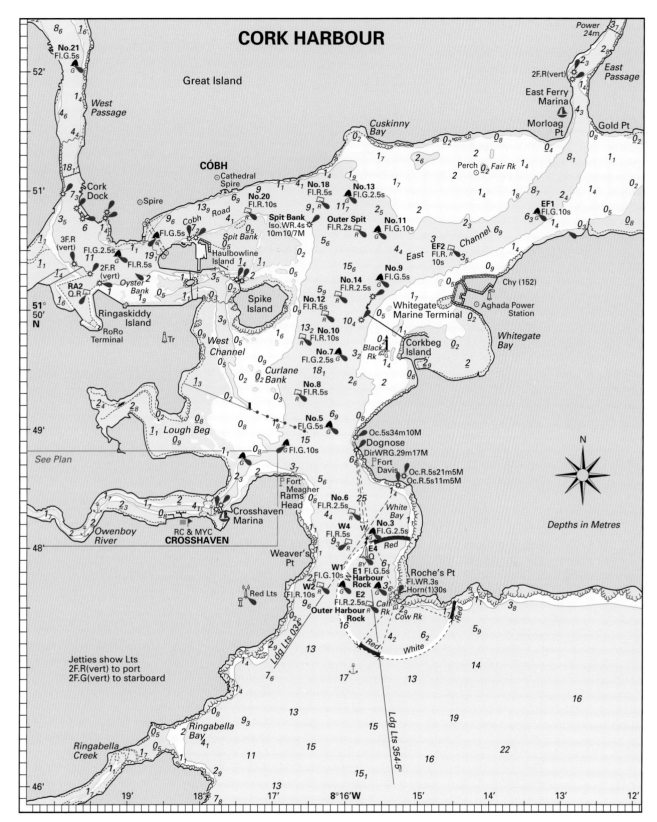

CORK HARBOUR

CROSSHAVEN

Crosshaven is the best harbour for a first arrival. This former British garrison village has grown little. In the sheltered Owenboy River, entered beyond Fort Meagher, it is now the home for a large number of yachts. It has two boatyards, three marinas, a 40-metre visitors' pontoon, moorings and a delightful anchorage upstream.

Shopping is limited but a small supermarket sells beer and spirits as well as wine, whilst Mr Kidney purveys excellent meat. The Royal Cork Yacht Club serves meals in the bar and dining room but does no food on Mondays. Pubs and restaurants abound in the village. Carrigaline, a disused

Cow & Calf Rocks | Roche's Point LH | Crosshaven | Fort Meagher | Fort Davis | Cóbh

Spike Island

Cork Lower Harbour

Roche's Point Automatic weather station

Cork lower harbour beyond Roche's Point from SE

port 7km upstream, has a large SuperValu. The regular bus service to Carrigaline from Crosshaven continues to Cork.

CROSSHAVEN PILOTAGE

Tides HW Cóbh

RNLI Inshore Lifeboat

Monitor Cork Harbour Radio on VHF 12. In poor visibility beware of ships waiting at anchor well outside Roche's Point. Arriving from seaward Cork's large Fairway Buoy (with Racon) is 5 miles southeast of Roche's Point. (A DF bearing of approximately 310° to Cork Airport's aero beacons – OC 343 or OB 362 – would get you within earshot of its whistle.) The buoy is just to the west of the main leading marks and sectored light (354°), on Dognose Point, for big ships. Ships from the west have another set of leading marks and lights (034°). Yachts can use all the wide entrance so these aids are not needed, though the channel buoys help gauge the streams. These are considerably modified by wind and heavy rains and run up to 3kn over the 'shallows' of Harbour Rock in the entrance and Turbot Bank beyond. The main hazard is angling boats ever on the move!

The channel into Crosshaven's narrow entrance is marked by lit lateral buoys, on a mean heading of about 250°. (The leading marks have been removed.) After the last PHM, in this direction, turn on to SW to pass

between a lit PHM and flashing green on a pier. There is a lit SHM guarding shallows to starboard inside the entrance, but after this many moored craft 'mark' the starboard side, leaving quite a narrow fairway. At night, rather than negotiate this congested channel, it is prudent to anchor outside – to the south of the approach channel. The marinas are not manned much before 0900. Be aware that many small boats, and some yachts, do not obey the collision regulations!

All marinas are to port. First is Crosshaven Boat Yard Marina, with water, AC, diesel and basic ablutions. Next is the 40m pontoon for angling boats and yachts, with a tap, below Town Quay. The inner side of this pontoon is *strictly* for the RNLI. There are toilets and an ice machine on the quay. Next is Salve Marine with excellent engineering services. This has a few pontoons suitable for very long yachts and a diesel berth on the long outside pontoon. Finally comes the Royal Cork Yacht Club's very large managed marina, with visitors' berth on the upstream section and a few visitors' moorings. Diesel can be delivered and possibly small amounts of petrol. There are scrubbing posts alongside a large slip. Yacht and dinghy racing is the main activity, with berthing for many cruising boats.

Upstream are many moorings but there is room to anchor in places – in deep holes with strong currents! The best anchorage is in wooded Drake's Pool 1½ miles upstream. This

has two pools joined by a shallow ledge. Moorings leave some space to anchor. Holding is good – when it can be found. It is difficult to land at a derelict quay so use a natural slip on the small promontory to the south of the lower pool. Tenders are stored here, and there is a grass area for BBQs. Carrigaline is 2½km along a riverside track. At HW a tender can tie up at a slip or an old sand quay just below the town.

CROSSHAVEN

The *Crosshaven Guide*, and much else, is available from the village's very helpful tourist booth outside the RCYC. The oldest part of Crosshaven surrounds The Square, overlooked by 18th-century Crosshaven House, which had a soup kitchen during the Great Famine. In the grounds are tennis courts and good pitch & putt golf. The supermarket, PO, bank and pharmacist are nearby, as is Cronin's Bar for very good bar lunches. Try the fish chowder with Thecla Cronin's soda bread. Take-away oysters (to order) are huge and cheap.

Crosshaven Boat Yard is where Sir Francis Chichester and Tim Severin had their very different craft – *Gypsy Moth IV* and *St Brendan* – built. It is still run by the family of the late Denis Doyle, veteran racer of *Moonraker*. This and adjoining Castle Point Boatyard can assist with shipwright and rigging problems.

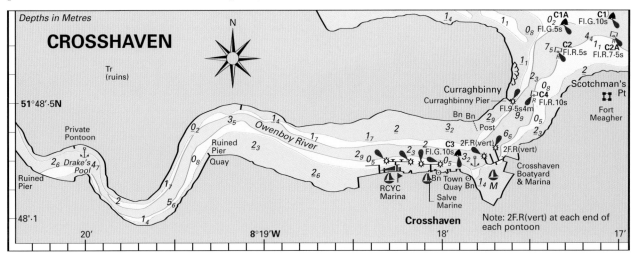

Drake's Pool from footpath and cycle track between Crosshaven and Carrigaline

Royal Cork Yacht Club is the long blue and white building, seen from the club's marina. RCYC is spelt out with flags

Drake's Pool, Owenboy River – looking upstream from Crosshaven

From Fort Meagher (named 'Camden' by the British) there are views over Spike Island, with its once notorious prison, to the old port of Cóbh. Thomas Meagher, an Irish patriot whose death sentence was commuted to transportation, later escaped from Australia to become a general in the Federal Army during the American Civil War. Beyond the fort a coastal footpath gives views to Roche's Point. The fort has a regular bus service from Crosshaven. Myrtleville, 3km south of Crosshaven, is like a sandy Cornish cove – with ice-creams, a very good general store, a bar and restaurant.

Angling and harbour trips can be arranged at the Schooner Bar, which is favoured by locals and has many photographs of the railway which once served the village.

The Royal Cork Yacht Club claims to be the oldest such club in the world. The Water Club of the Harbour of Cork was established on Haulbowline Island in 1720. Activities were mainly 'War Games', with the Admiral giving cannon and flag signals! In the 1800s the club moved to Cóbh, becoming the Cork Harbour Yacht Club and later the Cork Yacht Club. In 1831 King William IV bestowed the 'Royal' prefix. In the 1960s the club amalgamated with the Royal Munster Yacht Club and moved to Crosshaven. The clubhouse is not a grand building, but has been tastefully fitted out with all the usual

Path & cycleway to Carrigaline

Shallow ledge dividing upper and lower pool

Private pontoon

Derelict pier

Picnic area

Natural slip

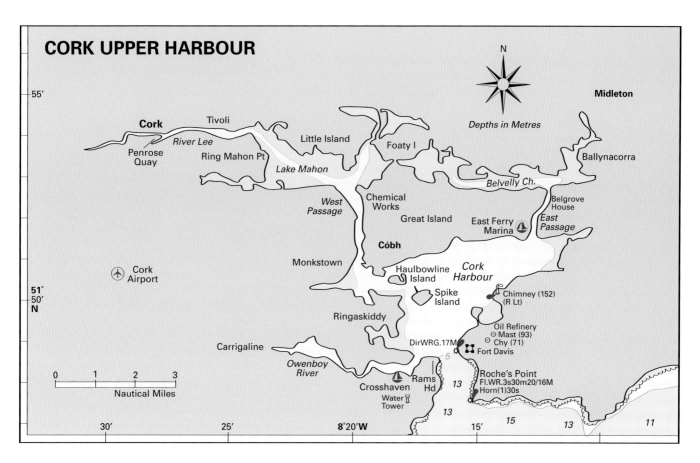

facilities. The RCYC hosts an international racing week biennially in even years. Details from www.royalcork.com

CORK UPPER HARBOUR

Cork was once a medieval walled port – 'Harbour Safe for Shipping' as its emblem proclaims – amongst the marshes above Great Island. (The Irish for 'marsh' sounds like 'Caarrrk'). On the tide it takes about 2½ hours from Crosshaven, but a fresh northerly should be avoided. Presently Penrose Quay, the last to starboard where the River Lee forks below the city, is the only berth for yachts. The Cork Docklands Project envisages more berthing for visiting yachts and cruise vessels along the city quays, with some provision for cargo vessels. Check with the harbourmaster if planning a visit as a Tall Ship can take all the available space on Penrose Quay. From the tourist office get the *Cork City Area Guide*, which has the best map of the city.

Cóbh's only usable berth is the Water's Edge Hotel's seasonal pontoon. This is next to what was The Cork Harbour Yacht Club, now the Sirius Arts Centre. The pier just east of this is for Spike Island's prison boats only. Opposite is Haulbowline Island, once a Royal Navy base; now the HQ of the Irish Naval Service. (Before a square rigger went about, the order was 'Haul bow lines'.)

The Sirius Centre has all the information on Cóbh and Great Island. Study this in the nearby Titanic Bar, overlooking the landing stage from which passengers boarded tenders for the ill-fated *Titanic* anchored outside Roche's Point. Close by is a newsagent which sells books about Cóbh. There is a regular train service to Cork, with good views of the waterway. Alight at Kent Station near Penrose Quay and Union Chandlery. For sailing information contact Eddie English, whose sailing school is in Cóbh: ☎ 021 4811237 *Email* info@sailcork.com Good accommodation for crews is at Bella Vista

Water's Edge Hotel's seasonal pontoon, Cóbh. The large cream building was The Cork Harbour Yacht Club; now the Sirius Arts Centre

Spike Island looking NW towards West Passage & Cork City

Cork Dockyard

West Passage

Lough Mahon

Water's Edge Hotel's seasonal pontoon

Haulbowline Island

Star-shaped fort and prison on Spike Island

The Orangery in Fota House's world famous arboretum, easily reached by train from Cóbh or tender/road from Belvelly Channel

Cork City

Little Island

Lough Mahon

Quays at West Passage used by freighters

Marino Point chemical works

Looking NW from West Passage towards Lough Mahon (which has a dredged channel) and Cork City

House Hotel (or at their Harleys B&B) ☎ 021 4812450 *Fax* +353 (0)21 4812215 *Email* info@bellavistahotel.ie www.bellavistahotel.ie

AC 1772 makes pilotage to beautiful East Passage, with its East Ferry marina, simple. But allow for strong cross tides in East Channel and do not visit on the ebb with a strong southeasterly. Gold Point is identified by the boulders which front it. East Ferry marina always has a contra-eddy so make a close pass before going alongside one of the long outside pontoons, which have at least 7m of water. As in other marinas, you will soon be greeted and allocated a suitable berth. Owner George Butler runs this secure marina, and his farm, almost single-handed. The safety of boats, and comfort of their crews, is his first priority. There is water and free AC, with no charge for drying alongside

The old Midleton Distillery – 'The Home of Jameson'

Anchorage 'behind the island' Midleton Channel to Ballynacorra

Ahenesk House Ballynacorra

Shallows rapidly

Moorings

East Ferry Marina

a quay or on the slip between tides. Arrange this by telephone on ☎ 021 4813390 (the bar) or ☎ 021 4811342 (George's home). There is no VHF and some mobiles do not work here. Diesel is always available. The showers and toilets were refurbished in 2005.

The marina has an excellent managed pub and restaurant (The Marlogue Inn) open from lunch to supper time almost everyday of the year. Patrons are always friendly, informative and entertaining. Besides sailors you will meet harbour pilots, members of the naval service, boat builders and harbourmasters as well as the general public.

A lift into Cóbh is often possible, with a taxi for the 7km of hills on return. Cóbh is one of the few seaside towns in Cork and Kerry where hire cars are easily arranged (see *Appendix*). SuperValu delivers to the marina. Walk the woods from your boat; you may see a red squirrel; now almost extinct in southern Britain. Ballymore, 3km from East Ferry, has

Aghada Pier Aghada Power Station Roche's Point Whitegate Marine Terminal

East Ferry Marina

Looking NE over East Passage from the marina to the old ferry pier and Murphs pub

Belgrove House with private pontoon

Old ferry pier with water tap and Murphs pub above

The Church of Ireland notice board give details of services

Marlogue Inn

Marina's quay and slip

Berths on Penrose Quay, Cork, on northern arm of the River Lee. Jurys Inn and a shopping mall are beyond Michael Collins Bridge

Belgrove House in East Passage with Trafalgar Tower. Waterloo Tower is now concealed by trees

St Finn Barre's Cathedral beyond South Gate Bridge and Sullivan's Quay, Cork

a pub with a take-away chippie next door. Join in the *craic* later in the evening.

The ferry across East Passage has been discontinued, but its wooden pier, on the eastern side, is in good condition. Used by fishing vessels, it is suitable for the average yacht, which may just touch at LW. There is a tap, but Murphs pub is just above for something stronger – and good grub too. From here to Roche's Point is easy cycling, passing an interesting old quay at Rostellan. Next is Lower Aghada, an American seaplane base in the First World War, which has a combined sailing and tennis club. The pubs and restaurants there are popular with local sailors who moor or go alongside the pier.

BACON AND CABBAGE

During our research for this book *Balair* has spent many happy hours at East Ferry Marina, looked after well by George Butler, all his staff and the many friends made there. They gave us many recipes for traditional Irish meals, and the more complicated ones were adapted to *Balair*'s limited galley. Bacon and Cabbage is now often enjoyed at home in west Cornwall – when it is Graham's turn to cook this delicious, but very easy dish!

Ingredients for 2–4 depending on appetites
1 green cabbage, quartered and broken into leaves
1 leek (or large onion), sliced
8oz streaky bacon (one lump is better than slices, and if salted soak for several hours)
⅓ pint of stock or water
Salt and pepper.
To cook

Line a heavy frying pan with half the bacon, then cover it with the cabbage and leek/onion and season. Put the remainder of the bacon on top and pour on stock (water will do if no stock or cubes available). Cover and simmer for precisely 1 hour. Serve hot.

To make a more filling dish, most people add whatever vegetables they have – potatoes, carrots, beans – with the cabbage and onion.

THE ANCHORAGE 'BEHIND THE ISLAND'

Past beautiful Belgrove House, with its Trafalgar and Waterloo Towers, Nelson's navy had a very secure anchorage above East Passage. This is marked on the chart and was also used by schooners awaiting the tide for Ballynacorra, the old port for Midleton. Holding is good just southwest of Ahenesk House. The flood tide here gives the tender a good initial push into and up the 2½ miles of Ballynacorra River for Midleton. The channel is first marked with intermittent white buoys, and then flows between meandering banks.

Warehouses on the east bank at the old port of Ballynacorra are converted into modern housing. The best landing place is a slip beyond these, keeping close to the quays. Jameson's Old Distillery is a short walk and is well worth a visit. Midleton, an important town, gets its name from being midway between Youghal and Cork. Shopping is excellent, with a small Tesco and large SuperValu. On Saturdays there is a very popular farmers' market. From the ferry pier by Murphs it is 7km by bicycle to Midleton. There is much else of interest in and around Great Island.

Yacht charter
See *Appendix*
Marine Services
See *Appendix*

CORK TO RINGABELLA BAY

Leaving the harbour there is now time to admire the two forts built by the British to keep out Napoleon. In morning sunlight Meagher is very impressive.

We are now entering West Cork with its slightly wilder landscape. Ringabella Bay, the first inlet just outside, has an anchorage at the mouth, south of a drying estuary – mainly used by day-sailors. There is a small store. Yachts normally pass inside Daunt Rock, with its PHM for large vessels.

ROBERTS COVE

Tides HW Cóbh

The very narrow entrance, just southwest of Cork Head, has a few moorings. It then shallows to a pretty beach with a nice pub. A small caravan park has a store. Quite big yachts visit this tiny haven. In settled weather

Roberts Cove with orange pub and stone arched bridge

Oyster Haven, from south

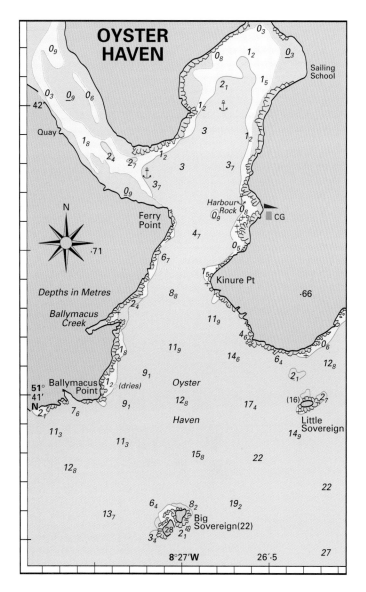

it is a lovely spot for a bilge-keeler to dry out. There is a tap at a nearby grass area for campers. The entrance is easily missed; from the east look for a bright orange pub with a stone arched bridge to its right. From the south, caravans and a mauve bungalow appear before the cove opens up. A bearing of 333° from Daunt Rock leads to the cove. The headland just south has a small building with a flat roof extending seawards.

ONWARD TO OYSTER HAVEN

Reannies Point has a modern look-out. Here the huge white pillars on the chart have weathered to a dark grey. Further on there are more, probably gateposts for a rare public right of way. Until just east of Oyster Haven the cliffs are undulating layers of slate – at a uniform height.

OYSTER HAVEN

Tides HW as Kinsale

This is a large unspoilt inlet. Early invaders from Scandinavia named it – not for oysters but as the haven east of Kinsale. When entering, keep south of Little Sovereign and clear of Harbour Rock (0.9m), which is opposite Ferry Point. There are moorings, with room to anchor, north of Ferry Point. A more exposed anchorage lies about two cables northwest of the slip by the cottages of Oyster Haven. Holding is good between

From the anchorage NW of the slip at Oyster Haven, with the Irish Coast Guard's white building

patches of weed. Irish Coast Guard have one of their strategically-based buildings here, used mainly to store equipment to combat oil pollution and for coastal rescue. Up the eastern arm of the inlet there is a sailing school and activity centre. A further 1½km by road or dinghy brings you to a restaurant at Ballinclashet. The nearest store and two pubs are at Nohaval – 6km by road. This is a haven for long explorations by dinghy, bicycle or on foot.

FINALLY TO KINSALE

From Oyster Haven to inside the entrance to Kinsale the coast slopes steeply towards the sea, with bracken-covered walled enclosures. There is room to go inside Big Sovereign, but keep well off Ballymacus Point, the western entrance to Oyster Haven. *Balair* passed inside Bulman Rock, at the eastern entrance to Kinsale, using a clearing transit – north side of Big Sovereign on with Frower Point (291°).

KINSALE

Kinsale Harbour is easy to enter at any tide and in any weather except with very strong winds from the south against a strong ebb, taking care at night. Just before the 17th-century Charles Fort there is a moderate bar with least depth 3m. Once in the westerly reach of the river Bandon there is complete shelter. There are two marinas, a possible alongside pontoon berth, moorings and upstream anchorages. Before these, Sandy Cove, north of its namesake island on the west side of the entrance, is a good anchorage – as is pretty Summer Cove opposite James Fort.

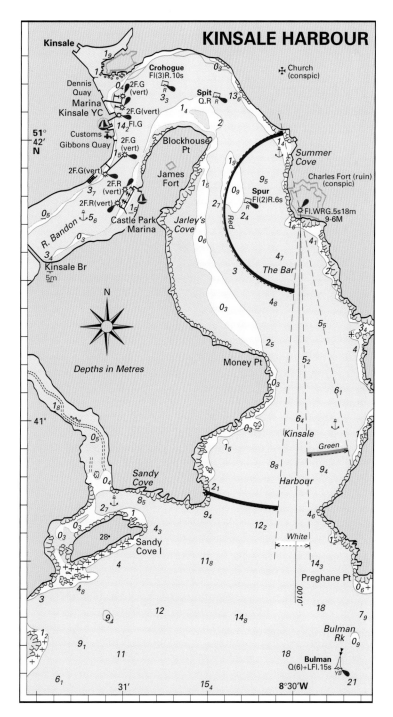

Sandy Cove anchorage, Kinsale, from S

Bridged Whitecastle Creek; the river is upstream to the west

Bandon River above the road bridge

Kinsale

Sandy Cove Village

The Pill

Anchorage

Although it is a busy fishing port with commercial traffic, Kinsale has every facility for the sailor. There is also easy cliff-top walking; little of this is to be found around the rest of West Cork and West Kerry. Old Head of Kinsale with its present and old lighthouses, castle, signal tower and well-preserved promontory fort, is worth a visit. The museum and guide books tell of the importance of Kinsale in Ireland's history; events of long ago still cast a shadow over Ireland's north.

An ugly low-level road bridge, with no lifting span, now crosses the river Bandon above the town, but a motor yacht can still explore this great river. Crews of heavily laden boats named the port Ceann Sáile (the 'head of the salt'). Their vessels might have foundered in that freshwater highway which stretches 15km inland unless they partly unloaded at Ceann Sáile.

The tourist office has all the information on this ancient historic port, which once extended to bonded warehouses in The Glen off Market Quay (now a road). Kinsale Harbour Commissioners' website www.irelandwide.com/port/kharbour/index. htm is also excellent (their email is kharbour@iol.ie). There is a SuperValu, other shopping and a self-service laundrette. Kinsale Yacht Club is very welcoming, with a modern extension to the original 18th-century building. Here there is excellent company, evening meals (except Monday, Tuesday and Friday) and showers. Hand your Visa card to the barman to pay the bill or to acquire shopping euros.

Local activities include good golf, riding, pony trekking, clay pigeon shooting and salmon fishing on the Bandon. A worthwhile trip is up this river to Bandon (part of the way by water or all the way by road), passing Shipool Castle below Innishannon, and Downdaniel Castle above, both on bends of this once strategic waterway. Walk the roads above the marina, lined with 18th-century

Anchorage off pretty Summer Cove, opposite James's Fort

An anchorage Castle Park Marina Trident Hotel and pontoons Kinsale Yacht Club's Marina

Old quay used by fishing vessels

Town Quay

Pontoon for fishing vessels only

James's Fort

Jarley's Cove

merchants' houses, and then take the circular walk around Compass Hill. You will see few tourists. Cork is only 25km by bus and Cork Airport is 18km.

Kinsale Chamber of Tourism website has complete information on the town and all its services: ☎ 021 4774026 *Fax* 021 4774438 *Email* info@kinsale-tourism.ie www.kinsale.ie

KINSALE PILOTAGE

Tides HW Cóbh –0015
Ebb up to 3kn, flood 1½kn
VHF HM/Port Control Ch 14. Monitor 14 for commercial traffic
RNLI Inshore Lifeboat at Kinsale Yacht Club Marina
Beware salmon drift nets

The leading light is obscured until west of Bulman SCM; the white sector is narrow so keep the light bearing 001° until Spur PHM comes on to the desired bearing.

Kinsale's marinas

Entering Kinsale from abeam Charles's Fort, Spit PHM is below the SE end of the multicoloured houses ahead

Scilly peninsula has good pubs and restaurants for sailors

SuperValu

Kinsale Yacht Club

Trident Hotel & pontoons

Town Quay

Kinsale Yacht Club's marina from S

On a visual approach do not let the scenery distract you from the chart! Keeping well to starboard avoids the shallows to port. The right end of a row of attached multi-coloured houses on the hillside ahead is above Spit PHM. Kinsale Yacht Club's excellent and secure marina (☎ 087 6787337 or www.kyc.ie) is for those completing a long passage; there is at least 11m of water. As usual go alongside or raft up on an outside pontoon until met. Beware of the very strong ebb.

Past this is Town Quay, used by large commercial vessels; after which is the glass-fronted Trident Hotel which has pontoons, for charter yachts, which may have a free berth. Ahead to starboard is a long pontoon strictly for fishing vessels, which also use an old quay and slip beyond. Just above this slip is a good anchorage, clear of strong currents and most traffic, abreast 3 white cottages. Holding is very good in shale and mud. Opposite is Castle Park Marina with moorings above towards the road bridge. The bridge has clearances between 5m and 8.7m

From the anchorage at Sandy Cove, on the western side of the entrance to Kinsale

on its southern side, with plenty of water at all tides.

Local boats use Castle Park Marina which is by an old oyster quay. This has new facilities and a free water-taxi to and from the town. Here it is peaceful (compared to the Kinsale side in high summer) with a family pub. A few yards away is Jarley's Cove, with bathing from a small beach. ☎ 021 4774959, website via www.ballyhasslakes.ie VHF 06, 37 (M), 16.

Yacht charter

See *Appendix*

The Dock overlooks Kinsale's Castlepark Marina

Kinsale Yacht Club

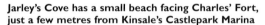

Jarley's Cove has a small beach facing Charles' Fort, just a few metres from Kinsale's Castlepark Marina

2 KINSALE TO CROOKHAVEN

Baltimore. The small fishing and ferry port looking towards Toe Head

2 KINSALE TO CROOKHAVEN

Ports, harbours and anchorages

Kinsale – Courtmacsherry – Clonakilty
Glandore/Union Hall – Castle Haven – Barloge Creek (Lough Hyne)
Baltimore – Sherkin Island – Ilen River
Cape Clear Island – Long Island Bay – Crookhaven
Goleen – Toormore Bay – Long Island Channel – Schull
Schull – Roaringwater Bay – Ballydehob
Through the Islands of Long Island Bay

Arrival ports
Baltimore Harbour or Kinsale

Charts and maps
Passage and planning charts
Imray C56, AC 2424

Essential large-scale charts
AC 1765, 2092, 2129, 2184
OSI Discovery Series Map 86, 87, 88, 89

Coastguard radio relay stations with working channels
Cork Ch 26
Mizen Ch 04

RNLI Lifeboats
Kinsale, Courtmacsherry, Baltimore

Important landfall lights
Old Head of Kinsale
Galley Head
Fastnet Rock

Tourist information
Cork Kerry Tourism, Aras Fáilte, Grand Parade, Cork
☎ 021 4273251 *Fax* 021 4273504
Email info@corkkerrytourism.ie

A BRIEF DESCRIPTION OF THE AREA

For the first taste of Southwest Ireland this area has everything. Many will arrive from the southwest and wish to start cruising from further north. Before returning they should, if possible, make time to cruise round or through the islands of Long Island Bay. As the gull flies it is 50 miles from Kinsale to Crookhaven. However, visiting the nine harbours, countless anchorages and exploring the many islands in this cruising area could take weeks! Cruising sailors who use this book sensibly will have the luxury of long days at anchor in this area, in lovely havens of their choice, relaxing and exploring at their leisure.

Kinsale is an excellent initial arrival harbour. Baltimore is more central but does not have quite such good facilities. The lovely natural harbour of Schull is only 7 miles of challenging pilotage through Carbery's Hundred Isles from Baltimore. It should be included in a cruise of this area as it also has good shopping. Then there are Roaringwater Bay, Long Island Channel and Toormore Bay; all with many secluded anchorages. (Do not let 'roaringwater' discourage you; that is the name of the river at its head.) Smuggling, far from the reach of the law, was a major 'industry' in West Cork. Whether Catholic or Protestant, priest or landlord, this was one

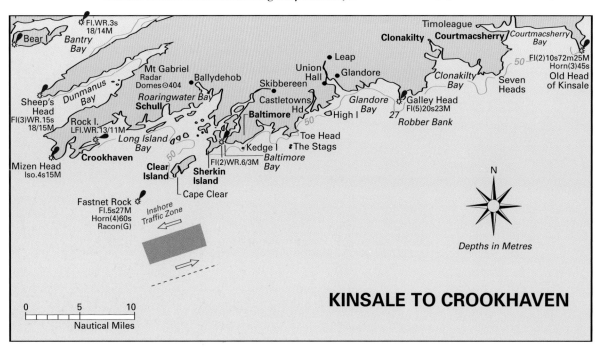

KINSALE TO CROOKHAVEN

occupation which united all! Fishing, mainly for pilchard and mackerel, was the mainstay of coastal communities and there was also much legitimate trade with France, Spain and Portugal, but fortunately there are no longer privateers from England, France or the Barbary Coast to carry off pressed men or slaves.

On the sailing routes from the Americas, Indies and Australasia a West Cork harbour was often the first port of call. Mail-boats called at Crookhaven, as did laden clippers 'for orders'. From the 18th century to 1938 the Royal Navy always kept a presence there. All have left their mark.

Another legacy was bequeathed by much earlier Celtic and Neolithic tribes – stone circles, wedge tombs, standing stones, ring forts and so on. OSI maps are littered with sites, but a hand-held GPS is needed to locate many of them.

There are no marinas west of Kinsale in this area, though you can walk ashore from pontoons at Courtmacsherry, Baltimore and Sherkin Island and from pier-side berths in Clonakilty and Cape Clear Island.

Kinsale is described in Section 1. Baltimore has shops, showers, diesel, gas, pubs and restaurants. A trip to Skibbereen, by bus or taxi, is needed to fully victual before proceeding to anywhere but Schull. Skibbereen by dinghy or bicycle from Oldcourt Boat Yard (3½ miles up the river Ilen) is an ideal excursion if weather-bound. Oldcourt is one of Baltimore's three boatyards. It has a deep-water pontoon (no charge for a day or so) and a pub.

Baltimore Harbour, like many in Cork and Kerry, is just a large bay (in this case not deep) between islands and the mainland. Entrance can be made from the south in any weather and with any tide, but only with caution at night. There are no visitors' moorings, but a sheltered anchorage can always be found. There is limited space for yachts on a serviced pontoon at Baltimore's small ferry and fishing port, with a similar berth at Sherkin Island, attached to the grounds of a new hotel offering showers.

KINSALE TO COURTMACSHERRY

From Kinsale, in fair conditions it is possible to sail close to The Old Head of Kinsale and peer through his neck to Holeopen Bay West from Holeopen Bay East. These caves are just south of the cliff-top castle. The chart shows a landing place in Gunhole Cove on the east side. A winding track leads up the cliff; could this have been to bring in materials for the light? There are two standing stones by the

lighthouse. From the west this wild headland is slightly marred by the clubhouse of a golf course.

The coast now shows all the signs of grinding ice and then continual battering from the seas. Many chunks are now coastal rocks and islands. The land generally gets lower with gently undulating hills running mainly westwards. The scrubby hinterland is often like that of West Cornwall, with occasional fertile fields sloping seawards to lovely strands.

COURTMACSHERRY

A local was once asked: 'What happens at Courtmac?' He replied: 'The tide comes in and then goes out.' It is still much the same. There is little for the holiday hordes, though many sea angling boats now come and go. For the discerning yachtsman who does not worry about shifting sand banks and strong currents it is an attractive place which gets little mention in the guidebooks. A pontoon gives wheelchair access to a village with a store, post office, pubs and restaurants strung along an estuary. There are easy walks beside this and in the surrounding countryside, or seniors can just relax whilst the new entry take sailing lessons, go canoeing or play tennis.

Courtmacsherry has the largest of five fortified coastguard buildings in the Republic. A detachment of the notorious 'Black & Tans' was based there, commanded by the man who fired Michael Collins's family homestead and later, as a senior officer, surrendered Singapore to the Japanese in the Second World War.

14th-century Franciscan Abbey at Timoleague, 2 miles up the estuary from Courtmacsherry

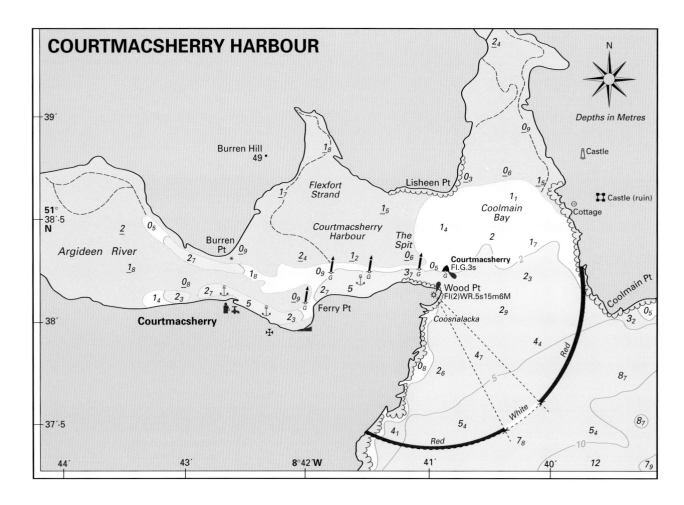

COURTMACSHERRY HARBOUR

Burren Hill
49 •

Flexfort
Strand

Lisheen Pt

Coolmain
Bay

Castle

Castle (ruin)

Cottage

39´

51°
38´·5
N

Argideen   River

Burren
Pt

Courtmacsherry
Harbour

The
Spit

Courtmacsherry
Fl.G.3s

Depths in Metres

Wood Pt
Fl(2)WR.5s15m6M

Coosnalacka

Courtmacsherry

Ferry Pt

Coolmain Pt

38´

37´·5

Red

White

Red

44´   43´   8°42´W   41´   40´   12

**Courtmacsherry,
looking E to Wood
Point and
Courtmacsherry
Bay**

Coolmaine Point

The Spit

Wood Point

Courtmacsherry

The Old
Coastguard

Town Quay

Visitors'
pontoon

Moorings &
anchorage

TIMOLEAGUE

Timoleague, 2 miles upstream, was an important trading port until an earthquake in 1755 silted up the whole estuary. AC2081 shows the channel for a dinghy trip to view the well-preserved shell of Timoleague's 14th-century Franciscan Abbey, but there is nowhere to land. An estuary-side footpath leads to this village, which has shops, pubs and ladies' hairdresser. Opposite 'Courtmac', Burren Point has a quay with access to roads around the saltings.

COURTMACSHERRY PILOTAGE

Tides HW Cóbh –0018
RNLI All-weather Trent

The harbour is entered by a tide-swept channel meandering through drying banks. Least depth is about 1.8m just past Ferry Point. Approach on 324° towards Wood Point sectored light; a night entry is not possible for strangers as the channel has only one other lit mark – a SHM at the entrance. Then there are starboard-hand spar buoys with moorings to port. Entry is dangerous in strong south to southeast winds. It is easier to approach near low water when breakers on The Spit allow. There is no VHF but HM/RNLI can assist on ☎ 023 46600.

The refurbished quay has a small pontoon, AC and nearby toilets. Diesel and water are on the quay, which has a good berth, but no ladder, across the seaward end. Yachts share the pontoon with a sailing school and angling boats. If anchoring, moor with two anchors from the bow, in the pool above the Severn all-weather lifeboat. In 1988, when *Balair* first visited this harbour, her new owners witnessed her, from a pub, dragging anchors laid from bow and stern. 'Don't worry, me dears,' came the cry. 'Someone will be after catching her for sure, so have another Murphy's!' In fact, she caught herself when free to face the currents.

CLONAKILTY

West of Courtmacsherry, Seven Heads has a prominent watch tower on Leganagh Point. There really are seven heads to this peninsula. Boats with moderate draught, which can take the ground, can enter the old port of Clonakilty ('Clon'). The bottom by the old steamer quay at North Ring is rocky and not suitable for lifting keels. Barytes were once mined here and exported by sea. 'Clon' was served by lighters loaded from ships at this quay when the upper harbour silted, probably after the 'quake of 1755. Only local boats use this and South Ring quay now. Clonakilty, a major West Cork shopping centre, is only 3km by road; the trip can also be made by dinghy. Land near Deassys Quay, as shown on the town's excellent website. At low water watch wading birds from the roads (built by famine labour) which completely surround the drying lough below the town. 'Clon' is a place for the adventurous, for golfers, game anglers, garden lovers and those interested in the birth of the Free State in the early 1920s.

Arriving in town by road or tender the first establishment is a large SuperValu with a coffee shop serving excellent meals. The town

Courtmacsherry

Moorings & anchorage

Visitors' pontoon

Good alongside berth but no ladder

RNLI all weather lifeboat

Fortified Coastguard

Tennis Club

Fishing vessel   Beacon

Even in light offshore winds there is surf on the beach at the entrance to Clonakilty. The fishing vessel has just passed Wind Rock Beacon

was settled by Protestants from England in the early 17th century. 'Clogh na Kylte' means 'Castle of the Woods'. These have long gone; it is now a very attractive and important market town. Out-of-keeping shop fronts have now been replaced with traditional ones and there are many reminders of the old brewing and linen industries. The Model Railway Village re-creates the now mainly defunct West Cork Railway. There is a food market every Thursday; look out for the famous Clonakilty black pudding. You can get *The Clonakilty, Rosscarbery, Timoleague and Courtmacsherry Visitors' Guide* from the Chamber of Tourism, Town Hall, Clonakilty, West Cork ☎ 023 35047 www.clonakilty.ie

In Clonakilty you will not be able to avoid hearing of Michael Collins. For his whole story see the commemorative edition of *The West Cork People,* published 22 August 2002.

Quay at North Ring, Clonakilty, from SSW

This is easy cycling country. Within a radius of 6km are Collins' birthplace and the village (with an exhibition of his cars) from which Henry Ford hailed. There is also very good game angling, golf and a famous garden – all on the same estate. As well as a fine stone circle there is a restored fortified Celtic farm. A touring caravan park (Desert House) is within walking distance of the town. Another (Sexton's), near Timoleague, is convenient for 'Courtmac' as well.

CLONAKILTY PILOTAGE

Tides HW as Courtmacsherry

If awaiting the tide, anchor in sand south of Ring Head. This is one of the few harbour when it is inadvisable to enter much before HW. On the extremely strong flood submerged moorings appear at high speed. It is essential to motor in. Approach from the middle of the bay, to avoid rocks on either side, and bring the right edge of the white hotel on Inchydoney Island on to about 330°. When the green tripod beacon on Wind Rock (dries 0.5) appears from behind Ring Head steer for it. This marks the starboard side of the narrow entrance, with the scoured edge of the beach to port. A conspicuous water-tower stands on high ground beyond. Even in light offshore winds there can be surf on this popular beach, so do not attempt entry in fresh onshore winds. A little further in, the beach extends as a shallow shifting bar. When past the beacon there are two attached cottages to starboard in a small bay. Go slightly to starboard here and keep about half

Approach to
Clonakilty, from S

Clonakilty

The second quay
at North Ring

South
Ring
quay

White hotel on
Inchydoney Island

Green tripod
beacon on Wind
Rock

Two attached
cottages

Ring Head

SuperValu

Road
from
Ring

Model Railway
Village

Tenders land in
cut below
Deassy's Quay

Clonakilty with
the road from
North Ring quay

A traditional
shop-front recalls
the old linen
industry

a cable off the shore. (The aerial photograph shows all the approach well.) The channel is scoured by the tides (to rock bottom, in places!) and gradually deepens to about 1.5m just before South Ring. Do not follow the shore here. It dries well out from South Ring quay so sound gently to port on to about 340°, between moorings, towards a second quay. There is a stony bar at the mouth of the creek just before this quay. At HW−0300 *Balair* found this on departure. Just above and east of this quay an eddy has scoured a hole, which probably shifts, of about 2.5–3m. A CQR held well here on ebb and flood, the boat just touching at times. The quay is in good condition with steps, a ladder, steamer bollards and a slip. Negotiate with the owners of many small boats before going alongside to dry out.

CLONAKILTY BLACK PUDDING DINNER

With thanks to Edward Twomey, butcher, Clonakilty, whose recipe this is based on.

Ingredients for 4
8 slices of Clonakilty black pudding (take Mr Twomey's advice on quantity)
4–6 potatoes
100g mushrooms (preferably wild)
2 dessert apples, peeled, cored, and cut into wedges
1tbsp vinegar (preferably sherry vinegar)
Knob of butter
2tbsp olive oil
Salt & pepper

To cook
Grate potatoes. Put into a bowl of water as you grate, then drain and squeeze out the excess moisture. Heat the olive oil in a frying pan, add grated potatoes and season to taste. Press into pan shape, allow to cook until nicely browned then turn over and cook on the other side. When completely cooked slide onto a warm plate and keep warm (in oven on low heat). Heat a little more oil and sauté the black pudding and mushrooms together for a few minutes. Remove from pan. Sauté the apples. Add the vinegar to apples, boil up the juices, add knob of butter and seasoning.

To serve
Place the pudding and mushrooms on the bed of potatoes, pour over the apples and juices. Cut the potato cake into wedges and serve.

Full Irish breakfast
A meal to last a day!
Conakilty black pudding cooked as above, plus:
Fried bread
Several slices of bacon
Fried eggs
Sausages
Tomatoes
Mushrooms

Edward Twomey the black pudding specialist
Joy Swanson

CLONAKILTY TO GLANDORE AND UNION HALL

DIRK BAY

There are no longer marks for the measured mile just east of Galley Head. However, 'Close to Galley Head, on its eastern side, is Dirk Bay, a small inlet about half of a mile in depth, where good anchorage may be obtained when the wind is westerly . . . on a fine sandy bottom.' (From *The Sailing Directions for the South, West & North Coasts of Ireland* (Imray, Laurie, Norie & Wilson Ltd, 1910)). *Balair*, battling homewards through the elements of late summer 2004, spent a comfortable night there in a fresh sou'westerly, anchored a cable off the slip shown on the chart in 2½ fathoms – half the depth suggested in 1910.

This inner bay has a restored house by the slip with a glass extension. ('Blow-ins' from mainland Europe like a view from their four-posters!) On the south side of the slip, used by local boats, are old fish-curing buildings. Apart from the 'glasshouse' it is very attractive. The foreshore is rocky with a small beach to the northwest. In the other corner of the bay is a bathing strand and caravan park. A road from the slip leads to the lighthouse, passing a castle, forts and a standing stone. This is also a useful anchorage for awaiting

Looking SW from the anchorage, sheltered by Galley Head, in Dirk Bay

Drombeg Stone circle, near Glandore, aligns with sunset at the winter solstice – in approximate direction of this photograph

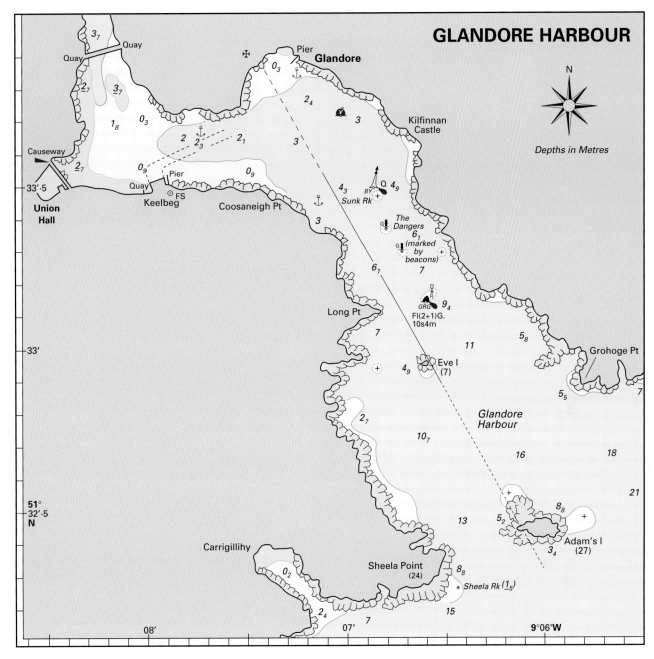

GLANDORE HARBOUR

Depths in Metres

daylight for Glandore's rock-strewn entrance, rather than using the much smaller Mill Cove or Tralong Bay just past Rosscarbery. Rosscarbery has no harbour, but a steamer quay which dries lies just inside Downeen Point, with anchorage off in 3m. (None of these anchorages was visited by boat.)

GLANDORE AND UNION HALL

Rounding Galley Head for Glandore, Doolic Rock and Sunk Rock lie half a mile off. It is safe to pass inside these rocks if conditions permit, keeping closer to the head, but there can be heavy seas here with wind against tide. Small islands and dangerous rocks start in earnest at Glandore: the first are in the entrance. Night approaches are only for fishing vessels and locals. This natural

harbour has everything for all yachtsmen, with visitors' moorings off Glandore's little curved pier which encloses a beach for toddlers. The pier has a landing pontoon for tenders and many sailing dinghies. In high summer Glandore, with its pubs and restaurants is overcrowded, but there are good walks to places of interest.

In the 19th century, a Dr Morris wrote:
'Of all the gems which deck our isle
And stud our native shore
None wears for me a sunny smile
As bright as sweet Glandore.'

Kieran O'Donague of The Glandore Inn (☎ 028 33468/33518 *Email* glandoreinn@ eircom.net) looks after the harbour and moorings. The hotel offers showers and has published a booklet of local walks.

Half a mile upstream, smaller boats can find anchorage, outside many moorings, off

Roury River for trout
& sea trout

Anchorage
(1.5m)

Slip

Quay

Mill Cove, two miles E of Glandore

Union Hall's large trawler quay. Prevailing winds tend to funnel down the creek above. Leave a fairway for large trawlers and show a light. This fishing village has good shops, a restaurant, pubs for fishermen and is not on the tourist circuit. Free showers are available on the quay by the harbour office. A helpful harbourmaster is always available on ☎ 028 3437, relayed to his mobile, and sometimes on VHF Ch 6 and 16. Yachts are welcome alongside, preferably at the eastern end, for fuel and water, when most of the trawlers are at sea. Diesel is from a tanker and water by hoses. Yachts can dry alongside the old pier to the east of the quay and tenders use the beach there. There is a very large slip and an ice machine, but the best

A salty pub at Union Hall

place for ice (and fish at wholesale price) is Ancar Fish Exports Ltd at the bottom of the main street. The curious name of the village stems from the hall built in 1801 to 'celebrate' the hated Act of Union between England and Ireland. Besides a small supermarket, there are two good hardware stores, with Kosan, Calor and Camping Gaz. On a Sunday local knowledge can be gleaned in the pubs from off-duty fishermen.

Dean Swift stayed at the village in 1623. Later, when sailing in *Laputa* he wrote the poem *Carberiae Rupes* (Rocks of Carbery) when storm-bound in our next port of call, Castle Haven.

It is not far to take the tender (with OSI 89) back to Glandore. Before exploring further visit the pretty church, approached through a rock tunnel, and ponder why it was so laboriously placed. At 1000 on Sundays in July and August there is a service. Well-excavated and documented Dromberg Stone Circle is a 4km hike. Adjacent are two hut circles and a *fulacht fia*; this was for cooking meat in water boiled by heated stones.

GLANDORE PILOTAGE

Tides HW Cobh –0025

Careful navigation is needed to find the entrance. Tidal streams are very weak. The channel has three dangerous rocks (The Dangers) along its centre, with Sunk Rock

Road to Drombeg
Stone Circle

The
Glandore
Inn

Church of
Ireland spire

Pier

Visitors'
moorings
and
anchorage

Glandore, from W

Limited
anchorage

Fairway for
trawlers

Harbourmaster,
showers and ice

Beach for
tenders

Slip

Road to Union
Hall – 0.5km

Yachts can dry alongside
the pier to the east of
the quay

Union Hall's Trawler Quay, with Glandore to the E

beyond. The preferred channel is to the west of these; strangers must use this. The Dangers are marked by three unlit beacons. A lit GRG buoy (preferred channel to port) is just seaward of a red post with basket on the southeastern Danger. This is the only PHM for the alternative channel. The next two Dangers have green posts and top marks. Sunk Rock is guarded by a lit NCM. It is not safe for strangers to enter at night. By day, leave larger Adam's Island well to port and head WNW towards much smaller Eve Island. (At first this is difficult to pick out against the eastern shore.) Leave Eve Island close to port and the GRG buoy will be ahead. The inbound track is now NNW with the east side of Eve aligned with the west side of Adam astern. A church with steeple lies dead ahead. After passing the NCM, head to the east of the church for visitors' moorings off Glandore pier or to anchor. If proceeding to the busy fishing village at Union Hall do not turn to port until the large concrete quay there bears 250° or less, to avoid a spit north of Coosaneigh Point. The anchorage off Glandore is not well sheltered from south to southeast winds. There is deep water between all the Dangers for those wishing to sail in or out!

GLANDORE TO CASTLE HAVEN

There is an inshore passage, passing south of dangerous Belly Rock off Rabbit Island and north of Seal Rock (which shows) just past Low Island, but the transits marked on AC 2092 pass very close to Belly Rock in the middle of the channel and very good visibility is needed to follow these. It is best to study the chart and use suitable bearings, eyeball pilotage and soundings to keep in safe water. *Balair*, piloted thus, first used the alternative departure channel, inside Adam's Island close to Sheela Point, and then gave Rabbit Island a good berth until approaching Low Island before turning for Horse Island outside Castle Haven.

CASTLE HAVEN AND CASTLETOWNSHEND

Castle Haven is a beautiful natural harbour with plenty of room for yachts to anchor off Castletownshend, named after the Townshends. This was an important trading port; the warehouses, old Coast Guard and

Stone row near Castletownshend. There was a fourth stone until a Somerville lady acquired it for the Castle gardens!

Map

CASTLE HAVEN

N

Depths in Metres

33'

51°32'N

31'

CP
Grassy Quay
Mill
The Narrows
Rineen River
Rineen
Castle (Ruin)
Spit
The League
Fort
Cat I
Tr
Slip & Quay
Castletownshend
Rineen Pier
Colonel's Rock
Castle Haven
(Ruin)
Reen Pt
Fl.WRG.10s 9m5-3M
The Battery
Skiddy I (9)
Green
Red
White
Flea Sound
Tracarta Pt
Horse I
Tr
Black Rk (21)

9°11'W

10'

The Castle – a 'modern' residence

Church of St Barrahane

Rineen River

Ruined castle

Anchorage above Cat Island

The League – always shows

Quay and slip

Cat Island

Rineen pier

Anchorage

quays are much as they were. Nowadays this neat 18th-century Anglo-Irish village is best known for the writings of Somerville and Ross (Edith Somerville and 'Martin Ross' (Violet Martin)). To learn all about them Gifford Lewis' *Somerville and Ross – The World of the Irish RM* (Viking Penguin) is available from British libraries. This tells of the brilliant writing partnership of two female cousins, and about life on land and water in Castletownshend and West Carbery during the late 19th and early 20th centuries. The church of St Barrahane, which is always open, tells even more about the Townshends and Somervilles. There is a well-stocked store which also sells stamps. The public telephone is useful as mobile reception is poor. Mary Ann opened her establishment in 1846; it is now a very good pub and restaurant. There is another restaurant, and Lil McCarthy's is a nicely modernised pub with a beer garden but no food. A plaque at the top of the village commemorates the Battle of Castle Haven which was linked with that of Kinsale. The castle at the harbour entrance has been recycled but another still stands guard up-stream.

Knockdrum stone fort is not shown on OSI 89 but is well worth a visit. The second gate on the left out of the village on the Skibbereen road has a sign. From the fort it is easy to spot the stone row shown on the map, whilst the views to seaward are sweeping. Beyond

the existing castle, on the Union Hall side, there is an interesting 'museum' on Céim Hill. The elderly owner, Therese O'Mahony, sells an interesting autobiography with tales of local characters.

The creek upstream is known as the Rineen River. A large water-mill at Rineen only recently ceased grinding grain. Take the tender during the long HW stand of such creeks. Keep close to the wooded promontory with the car park (shown on OSI 89) then parallel the road, rounding a reef marked on the map by small islands. A low grass quay lies ahead. To see the mill proceed to Rineen Cross Roads and then take the track off to the left. It is possible to view the mill from the water by keeping south of the reef.

Castle Haven with Castletownshend, looking NW

The large water-mill at the head of the Rineen River, Castle Haven

CASTLE HAVEN PILOTAGE

Tides HW Cobh –0025

The sectored light on Reen Point assists fishing vessels and locals to locate the entrance. Head up the centre of the haven. Beware of Colonel's Rock just inside Reen Point if beating. There are no visitors' moorings. Anchor southeast of Castletownshend quay clear of an underwater cable. Holding is not good, nor comfortable in strong southerly winds. There is limited room to anchor, in thick mud, in the sheltered deep channel between moorings above Cat Island. Show a light in either anchorage as fishing vessels move all night. The pontoon here is private so use the slip by the quay for landing. There is a tap with rubbish disposal there. Rineen pier is for fishing vessels.

CASTLE HAVEN TO BARLOGE CREEK

On leaving Castle Haven the tower you see on Horse Island to starboard was built by Thomas Somerville as a day mark for his returning merchantmen. Now round Black Rock for Toe Head; when viewed from the west this is aptly named as it looks like a reptilian toe complete with nail. The multicoloured layers of rock in the cliffs of Toe Head show all the actual colours of old red sandstone.

If not visiting Castle Haven the direct passage between Galley Head and Toe Head is clear of offshore dangers, except The Stags, a group of high-pointed offshore rocks. From the east these look like a schooner with black sails. The sound between The Stags and Toe Head is 6 cables wide and can be used safely

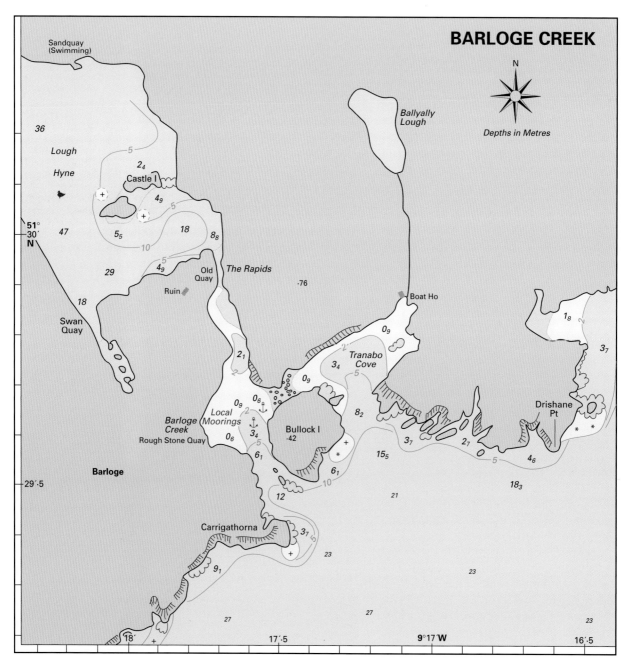

Base of Knockomagh · Sandquay · University College Cork's marine laboratory · Castle Island · The Rapids at slack water · Rough stone quay · Sheltered shallow anchorage · Drying Spit · Deep anchorage · Bullock Island with a thin thatch of conifers · Rock

by yachts. However, tides can run up to 2½knots. Outside a SCM guards the wreck of the MV *Kowloon Bridge*.

BARLOGE CREEK AND LOUGH HYNE

Barloge (hard 'g') with unique Lough Hyne ('Ine') lies 15 miles west of the Toe. In good visibility Barloge Creek is easy to find as it is backed by high, rounded and pine-covered Knockomagh. Closing Bullock Island, which has a thin thatch of conifers, the correct entrance is difficult to pick out. At HW a rock close to Bullock indicates a false passage between it and this island. Close in, small craft on moorings will show beyond the true entrance. This is a beautiful anchorage; a family of otters plays below The Rapids. You may be offered lobsters by the owner of a 100-year-old open black boat. Lough Hyne's entrance dries 3m and the sea is always running in or out, except at slack water, when it is easy to row through to explore the lough briefly. Beware of long weed and the reef off Castle Island if using an outboard. It is not possible to predict slack water in The Rapids so anchor or tie up below, before local HW, taking care not to be drawn down into rough water. When the white water stops let the tide take you in. During each tide cycle water

flows into the lough for 4 hours but cascades out, at up to 9 knots, for 8½ hours. As no significant fresh water feeds the lough it is full of clean, well-oxygenated salt water supporting several thousand species of marine animals and plants. University College Cork has a marine laboratory by The Rapids. At the top end of Hyne is a well-preserved sandboat quay. The university permits swimming from this, but beware of the Mediterranean purple sea-urchin's spines! In the 18th and 19th centuries the lough also supported a herring fishery. From the creek scramble ashore on the rough stone quay to view the lough, though the land to The Rapids is strictly private. Baltimore Harbour and 'Carbery's Hundred Isles' can be surveyed from the summit of Knockomagh.

BARLOGE CREEK PILOTAGE

Tides HW Cobh –0025
Streams inside are negligible, apart from The Rapids. Keep to port when entering to avoid rocks off Bullock Island. The recommended anchorage to the west of Bullock has about 4m, but shallow-draught boats can anchor closer to the drying shingle bar between Bullock and the shore with a view up to The Rapids. Holding is good clear of visible weed. In late summer, shrimp pots on sunken lines are set with just one buoy.

Barloge Creek with Lough Hyne beyond, from S. The gap between the rock and Bullock Island looks like the entrance from a distance

BARLOGE CREEK TO BALTIMORE

From Barloge to Baltimore the cliffs become high and more rugged again. The 19th-century signal tower to the southeast of Baltimore town will be a daymark throughout the rest of this area. 'See through' Kedge Islands off Spain Point have a narrow inside passage used by FVs and local yachts, avoiding the strong tides and possible overfalls outside. *Balair* took the outside option.

The tide is rising, but it is still ebbing out of Lough Hyne

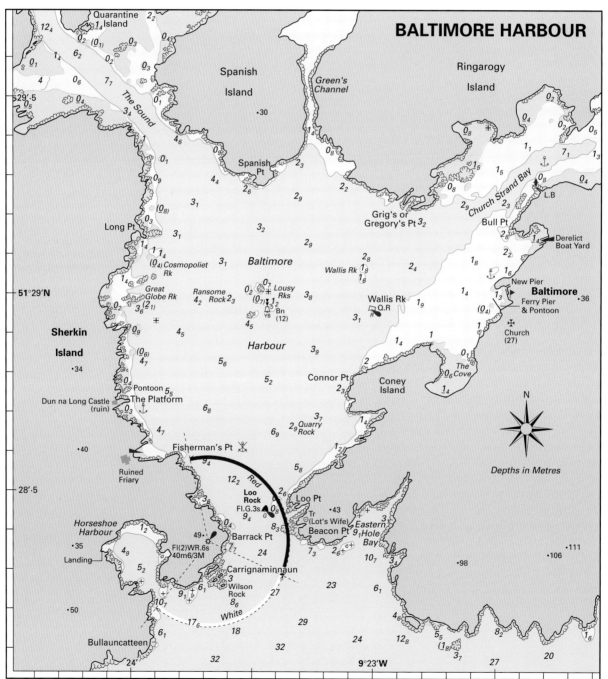

BALTIMORE HARBOUR

BALTIMORE HARBOUR

The harbour is relatively shallow, with several anchorages and two visitors' pontoons. For those choosing to anchor there is a water tap on the fishing vessel pier by the ice machine. Atlantic Boat Services (ABS) VHF 6, ☎ 021 774 958 *Email* info@atlanticboat.ie www.atlanticboat.ie have a secure visitors' pontoon on the ferry pier, accommodating up to 20 yachts, with AC and water. Fuel and gas can be arranged. Maximum length is 15m. Showers can be obtained from ABS, the friendly sailing club which closes at the end of August, Bushes Bar and Glenans Sailing School. Bushes, above the quays, can supply charts. There is some chandlery available, but Skibbereen has a very well stocked chandlery. ABS also has a chandlery in Skibbereen.

French-owned and staffed, La Jolie Brise is a good place to eat. Do not be influenced by the take-away sign; it is no cheaper than dining in this family-style bistro. Besides the usual 'full Irish breakfast', you can also have a 'hot smoked salmon breakfast'. A small supermarket sells most foods except meat.

For the other pontoon see Sherkin Island below.

BALTIMORE HARBOUR PILOTAGE

Tides HW Cóbh –0015
VHF Listen on Ch 6 for HM and Cape Clear Ferry. Others use Ch 9.
RNLI Offshore Tyne

With two entrances, streams and times vary. The main entrance is to the south between the lighthouse at Barrack Point on the west side and a tall white daymark (Lot's Wife) on the mainland. Enter on a northerly heading. Just inside the entrance, which is about 90 yards wide, is Loo Rock marked by a lit SHM. Leave this on NE towards the only other lit buoy, a PHM guarding Wallis Rock. Anchor to WSW or N of the small artificial fishing and ferry port. There is another well-sheltered anchorage with many moorings in 1.5m to 2m clear of the fairway northwest of the RNLI station's slipway on Bull Point. Many ferries and fishing vessels use the harbour, so always show a riding light.

Baltimore Harbour is relatively shallow. This unlit south cardinal marks Lousy Rocks, just north of the track between Baltimore ferry harbour and the ferry quay on Sherkin Island

Baltimore Harbour, southern entrance, from SE

Roaringwater Bay

River Ilen

River Ilen anchorage

Baltimore's small artificial fishing and ferry port

Spanish Island

Ringarogy Island

Lot's Wife daymark

Loo Rock SHM

Beacon Point

LH on Barrack Point, Sherkin Island

Baltimore's small artificial fishing and ferry port

Glenans Sailing School

Steps below water tap and ice machine

Baltimore Sailing Club

Shops, pubs & restaurants

Convenient anchorage

Slip

Fishing vessel quay

Visitors' pontoon off ferry pier

SHERKIN ISLAND

Balair later sheltered from a fresh north-westerly, at anchor between the island's new landing quay and the O'Driscoll Castle, a ruin in the grounds of the Islanders Rest. This hotel (☎ 028 20116 *Email* info@islandersrest.ie www.islandersrest.ie) has a pontoon with water and showers for patrons, but there is no waste-disposal facility. In this roadstead, looking southeast towards Lot's Wife, holding was good in 4m. There are steps on the north side of the pier clear of ferry traffic. The pier has a tap and notice-board guide to the island. Just above the landing place is a Franciscan Friary dating from 1460 which is being restored. Dun na Long Castle (the Fort of the Ships) is about the same age.

HORSESHOE HARBOUR

This is a delightful anchorage on Sherkin with an entrance facing southeast behind Barrack Point. Head in on about 315° towards the cluster of houses on the far side of the harbour. Approaching the 50-yard wide entrance keep to the southwest; when inside keep close to the east side. It is easiest near LW when the reefs show. (At anchor in sand the scenery in early May was beautiful.) There is a landing place on a small beach, just to the right of steps in the rock, below a white cottage in the northwest corner. On the other side of the island is shallow Kinish harbour with a rock-strewn entrance facing northwest. This is best left for local boats.

Franciscan Friary and Sherkin Island's pier with *Balair* anchored off

Sherkin has two lovely strands and a small beach, all facing Long Island Bay. Gentle walks to these are mainly through leafy lanes. There is a PO/store with Kos, and the lively Jolly Roger complements the modern bar at the hotel. Sherkin Island Marine Station, on the northwest corner of the island past Silver Strand, promotes awareness of natural resources, their use and protection. (It is not open to casual visitors.) Its conspicuous buildings make a good mark when departing westwards from Baltimore's northern entrance. The station has a very good website via www.homepage.eircom.net

RIVER ILEN TO OLDCOURT AND SKIBBEREEN

Tides
HW Oldcourt and Skibbereen approximately HW Baltimore +0030, heights similar to Baltimore

Large sailing vessels and later steamers used to go up the river to Oldcourt, trans-shipping cargo on to lighters for Skibbereen. Take the north exit from Baltimore Harbour through The Sound, between Spanish Island and Sherkin. Before making the passage to Oldcourt determine the track and distance of each leg. The low islands, which comprise most of the 'banks' are featureless and the

Southern entrance to Baltimore Harbour with Lot's Wife, on Beacon Point, silhouetted against a summer sunrise

Northern entrance to Baltimore Harbour

Sherkin Marine Station

Kinish Harbour

Jolly Roger

Traveller's Rest

PO and store

Visitors' Pontoon

Sherkin Ferry

Franciscan Friary

Best landing

Barrack Point

Horseshoe Harbour, Sherkin Island, from S

next course is not always obvious. A rising half-tide makes it easier to pick out the smaller islands, rocks and edges of the channel. If taking an anchorage en route HW–0200 is the ideal start time, but this is a bit late if proceeding all the way to Oldcourt.

Keep to mid-channel through The Sound, continuing on the same heading to midway between Sandy and Quarantine Islands. (If exiting this way ignore the warning of overhead cables ahead on Sandy Island. These have been removed, but in 2003 the notice had not.) There are moorings in the deep channel upstream north of Quarantine and the chart shows an anchorage – from the days of sail.

From Sandy Island *Balair* headed for Inane Point on Ringarogy Island, then followed the channel as shown on the chart, staying in the best water by sounder and on the outside of bends. As in most creek-crawling, the OSI map gives a good indication of the river bed; boulders lurk in the shallow margins. The anchorage on the chart opposite Inane Creek is uninviting. There is a quay with a large, modernised building (with another glass bedroom!) at the entrance to the creek. This could have been where grain was stored for export to England, whilst the local population was starving to death during the Great Famine.

Balair passed a couple of breezy days, anchored in mud, at the western end of the long reach north of Inishbeg. This was opposite a slip and old rectory at Reena Bhuna – with an ivy-clad ruined church just upstream. (GPS put this anchorage at 51°31′.5N 09°22′.0W.) A network of roads on the mainland side lead to Roaringwater Bay and a store at Church Cross – on the N71 6½km west of Skibbereen. A bus passes there for 'Skibb'.

On the final run to Oldcourt the channel around the bend northeast of Inishbeg has a shallow spot just past the slip to starboard. After the slip turn gently to port, passing close to a long pontoon to starboard, then turn NE for moorings on the outside of the next bend. After this bend Oldcourt Boatyard, with a castle to starboard, lies ahead. The deep-water pontoon (barge) is up-stream of the travel-lift dock, which has a drying waiting pontoon.

At Oldcourt Donal O'Donovan makes no charge for a few days alongside. The yard has a 70-ton boat hoist, a large hard with full boatyard facilities and a slip for small commercial vessels. Marine engines can be serviced. Contact Donal at Oldcourt Boats Ltd, Oldcourt, Skibbereen, Co Cork ☎ 028 21249 *Fax* 028 22277.

Hegarty's yard, opposite across a creek, restores historic craft, large and small. Old

Oldcourt Boatyard, River Ilen, looking NE upstream

Moorings well to port on outside of final bend

Skibbereen

Oldcourt Boatyard

The long pontoon to starboard

Court Inn is a family pub (which serves no meals), with a beer-garden facing the river and castle. Fishermen from Barloge Creek are customers. It is a very good place to be when the wind is storm force!

SHOPPING BY WATER IN SKIBBEREEN

Donal suggests taking a tender up to 'Skibb' not before HW–0300. This gives ample water to avoid the mud flats to starboard on the first bend, but not enough to cover stranded fallen trees. Just above Oldcourt there is an active rowing club with many championships under its oars. The club has laid a line of small buoys (not joined) along the centre of the river. This is to guide the scullers, not to mark the best water. These buoys end at a mid-stream island with dinghy water on either side. There is a quay to starboard here; on the upstream side of this a small motor yacht could tie up by the road. (This is 1½km from Skibbereen.) Now there are lush meadows to starboard and low rocky escarpments to port. Abbeystrowry ('Monastery of the Stream') graveyard, where thousands of famine victims were buried in pits, is to port below an arched bridge. A visit by road to this cemetery is recommended. The fairly narrow arches of the bridge have about 3m clearance at HW. The next road and old railway bridges in 'Skibb' are too low for a small motor cruiser. Just below on the east bank is a grassy bank with town access. Using anchors or stakes she could be secured here – for an hour or so around HW. To

Visiting yachts alongside the deep-water pontoon at Oldcourt

Levis's Quay, Skibbereen, has slippery steps and unsafe handrail

Abbeystrowry burial ground, where thousands of famine victims were buried in mass graves. Famine coffins had a hinged floor so that they could be reused

A MILLION A DECADE! - OF HUMAN WRECKS,
CORPSES LYING IN FEVER SHEDS -
CORPSES HUDDLED ON FOUNDERING DECKS,
AND SHROUDLESS DEAD ON THEIR ROCKY BEDS;
NERVE AND MUSCLE, AND HEART AND BRAIN,
LOST TO IRELAND - LOST IN VAIN.

PAUSE - AND YOU CAN ALMOST HEAR
THE SOUNDS ECHO DOWN THE AGES:
THE CREAK OF THE BURIAL CART,
THE RATTLE OF THE HINGED-COFFIN DOOR,
THE SIGH OF SPADE ON EARTH,
NOW AND AGAIN, ALL DAY LONG.

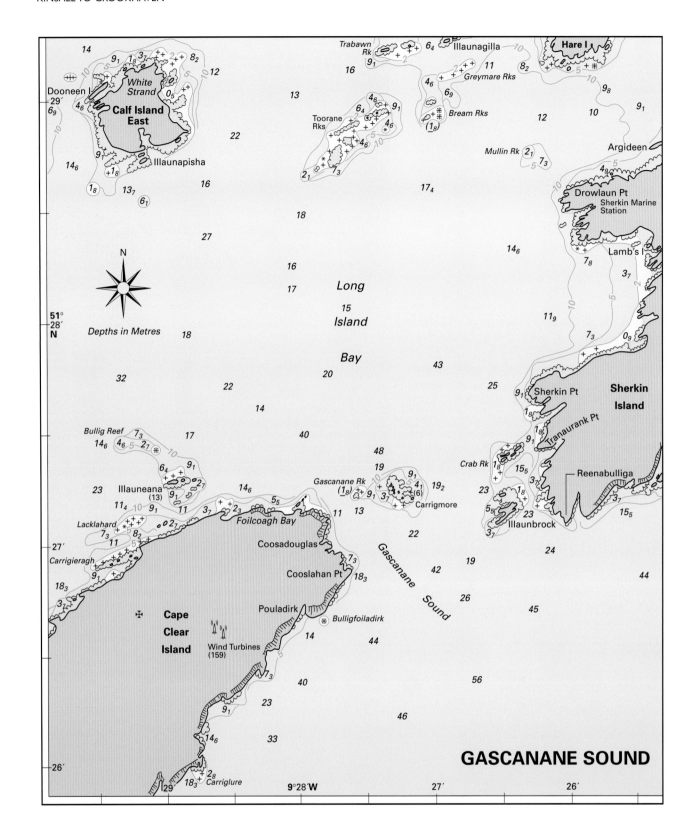

GASCANANE SOUND

starboard, just above the road and rail bridges, is a small cut and Levy's Quay, which has very old and slippery steps. The handrail is sufficient for securing to, but gives no support for disembarking! Above the steps a shop stocks Gaz, with a large SuperValu a few yards further on. The road north over the river leads to a good visitor centre describing the horrors of the Great Famine and natural history of Lough Hyne. (Ine is only 3km by road from Oldcourt.) 'Skibb' has a very good chandlery for yachtsmen and fishermen which also services life-rafts. See *Appendix*.

By Levi's Quay is an Auxiliary Warehouse, used by the destitute during the famine. A stand until HW+0200 gives ample time for shopping, eating or exploring. At HW most of the stranded trees are covered, but the black spots in the river marked on OSI 89 are not rocks! 'Skibb' is 4km by a riverside road from Oldcourt.

BALTIMORE TO CAPE CLEAR ISLAND

Tidal streams in Gascanane Sound
NW starts HW Cóbh –0055 at up to 3kn
SE starts HW Cóbh +0520 at up to 3kn

From Baltimore, a visit to North Harbour on Cape Clear Island or on to Crookhaven is a good plan before mixing it with the islands. The easiest route is through Gascanane Sound, between Sherkin and Cape Clear Islands.

Use the east channel as it is wider and a good deal deeper. From Gascanane head NW to clear Bullig reef before setting course for North Harbour on (Cape) Clear Island or for Crookhaven. The signal tower southeast of Baltimore bearing 082° clears Bullig.

The alternative route is from Baltimore's north entrance, going around Sandy Island then south of Hare Island, following the directions in the ICP (if you have it) read in reverse. ISDs give more comprehensive directions for this exit, again in the reverse direction. At half-tide most of the hazards can be seen. To avoid Mealbeg off Turk Head keep close to the line between the north points of Sandy Island and The Catalogues. From Turk Head to the deep channel between The Catalogues and Two Women's Rock, pilotage is by eye, bearing and sounder, making sure to go well to the northwest of Turk Head before turning port onto a southerly heading. Then identify Drowlaun Point, on the northwest tip of Sherkin, 'marked' by the white buildings of the Marine Station. Line up this point with the highest eastern point of Clear (Mount Lahan) on 213° to just clear the dangerous rock 3 cables south of Two Women's Rock. Keep to port of this clearing transit initially. Then pick up (if you can) Doonanore Castle on the northwest shore of Clear. This is on a low island which looks like a spit; line this up with difficult-to-see Illauneana Islands just off the coast of Clear Island on a bearing of 230°. In practice, it is easier to line up the northwest coast of Clear, keeping close in to Drowlaun Point. If you can see the Fastnet winking you are too far north!

Past Drowlaun Point you are clear of Mullin Rock. If not sure, wait until the eastern channel of Gascanane Sound is well open. Now proceed north around Bullig Reef.

The Bill of Clear and Cape Clear from NW

Doonanore Castle with Cape Clear Island's old signal tower and lighthouse beyond, from WNW

CAPE CLEAR ISLAND

Clear Island (Oileán Chléire) is beautiful and unspoilt. If you can not make it by boat take the ferry from Baltimore or Schull.

The island is 5km by 2km, with views over the archipelago of Long Island Bay to the Mizen peninsula, back to Baltimore and out to the Fastnet Rock. The island has an important bird observatory as it is on a migratory route. The population of about 140 (in 2004) depends mainly on the sea and farming for a living. The language is Irish as Clear is part of the Gaeltacht (see *Introduction*), but there is no trouble ordering a meal or a glass of the 'black stuff' at Danny Mikes, the islanders' pub. In the tourist season other pubs open.

North Harbour, Cape Clear Island. *Balair* **alongside in the inner harbour, beyond the tyres for the ferry's bad-weather berth**

NORTH HARBOUR

For a short visit to the island's North Harbour, berth on the inside of the outer breakwater; a favourite lunch stop for local yachts with rafting room for up to three boats. For a longer stay dry out on the northwest side of the central pier in the inner harbour. Petrol and green diesel are available by can from the Co-op on the west side of the harbour, which is open all year. This has helpful staff with email, photocopier, guide books and maps. Water is from a quayside tap by the small ice plant on the north side of this harbour. For fresh milk and bread await the morning ferry delivery to the well-stocked shop. Unusually, rubbish disposal is easy and there is a bottle bank.

NORTH HARBOUR PILOTAGE

Tides HW Cóbh –0025

Approach the narrow entrance on 196°. Keep clear of the east side approaching the harbour. There is 2m at the head of the central pier which is the ferry berth. Go alongside beyond this and dry out. At mid-tide there is enough water to enter the second inner harbour. Keep the main pier close to port for best water. Climb the tyres at the bad-weather berth for the ferry then work the boat forward. This is the best place for a long stay as many craft make day visits to the main harbour. Awaiting the tide, go alongside the end of the outer breakwater. There is a slip in the main harbour.

Calf Islands

196°

Ice and water

Ferry
berth

Co-op

Ferry bad-
weather berth
in inner
harbour

Shop

**Cape Clear Island.
North Harbour
from SE**

Ferry bad-
weather
berth

Co-op with
fuel pumps

Bird
Observatory

Water and
ice

Steps

Visiting yachts
rafted at the end of
the outer
breakwater

Shop

SOUTH HARBOUR

Balair did not coast the southern side of the island, but Cape Clear, from The Bill of Cape Clear to the entrance to South Harbour, is awe-inspiring. The Atlantic has chewed great lumps from the cliffs and carved deep caverns. It is far more fearsome than England's Lizard or Land's End, except that the nearest offshore rock is the Fastnet and the streams are not so fierce. The outer part of South Harbour has the usual sprinkling of pots. The entrance to the inner anchorage is a cable wide. In a light northwesterly this was a beautiful, but possibly weedy, anchorage. With any southerly swell it is not to be recommended. Abreast the quay there is plenty of room to swing on a long scope.

The quay connects with the roads along the spine of the island and to the signal tower and adjacent old lighthouse. (This was replaced by the light on the Fastnet Rock because it was often obscured by cloud.) A disused telegraph station is near the quay. It is a short walk over the neck leading to North Harbour, passing Danny Mikes on the way.

South Harbour is best for a day of exploration at springs whilst awaiting the evening tide for North Harbour. Proceeding back around Cape Clear, note that Doonanore Castle is now conspicuous, though it is a poor clearing mark when approaching the island from the northeast.

Inner harbour of North Harbour, Cape Clear Island

Cape Clear Island. South Harbour from NW

Disused telegraph station – road leads to the old lighthouse & watch tower

Quay

Danny Mikes

ON TO CROOKHAVEN

Crookhaven is the last harbour south of Mizen Head. The lighthouse and the buildings on Crookhaven's Rock Island look, from a distance, like a lightship facing west. The Calf Islands have a few derelict cottages and some attractive, but rock-bound, beaches. From the heights of Cape Clear Island the 'Calves' looked like cow pats! Past these is a good time to identify several useful navigational marks. The tall white tower on Copper Point at the eastern end of Long Island will have the very conspicuous Barnacleeve Gap behind it. The gap is just to the east of two silver radomes on Mount Gabriel. Leamcon Tower, west of Schull, will be to the northwest, with the castle on Castle Point further west at the entrance to Toormore Bay. Ruined Leamcon House was the destination for much contraband, though the occupant should have been on the side of the law! Battles with privateers were also fought in the channel here; note Gun Point at the entrance to Croagh Bay. On Brow Head, just west of Crookhaven, is a signal tower which could communicate with the tower on Bear Island to the northwest, with those on Cape Clear Island and at Baltimore, and so on round the coasts. These were built during the Napoleonic wars. In the days of sail, transatlantic boats delivered mail to Crookhaven, laden clippers called there 'for orders' and it was much used by the British Navy. So Lloyds built a signal station on Brow Head; later Marconi set up one of his chain of experimental radio stations there, ostensibly to find the best location for radio telegraphy to shipping – but secretly a reliable transatlantic radio station. Sir Thomas Cooke founded Crookhaven, as he did Baltimore, as a Protestant fishing village. Catholics in Crookhaven still have to travel a long way for mass!

CROOKHAVEN

'Crook' is a friendly place, with a sailing club offering showers, though the village gets overcrowded in high summer. The O'Sullivans have a store, post office and bar serving good food. Their pub is by a tiny dock with a beach safe for children.

Take the tender to White Strand and climb 1½km to Brow Head which also has the remains of a Cornish miner's village. The tidal lough behind Barley Cove has many species of wading birds. A wilder walk is along the seaward coast of Crookhaven with sheep, sea-birds and seals for company as you negotiate the deserted lazy beds. These were fertilized with sea-sand, seaweed, animal and human manure to grow the staple food (potatoes), to be boiled and washed down with buttermilk.

Rock Island is worth exploring. Land by an old pier shown on the photograph. Nearby are the remains of a lobster farm with broken sea-water pens. This was developed in the 1920s by a Frenchman for his home market. Some of the buildings on Rock Island were erected for workers on the second Fastnet lighthouse. The first iron lighthouse lasted from 1854 to 1881. The second (and present) one, of granite shaped in Cornwall into interlocking blocks, first showed a light in 1903. All the buildings on Rock Island are now private residences but a public road leads to a good viewpoint across to Black Horse Rocks.

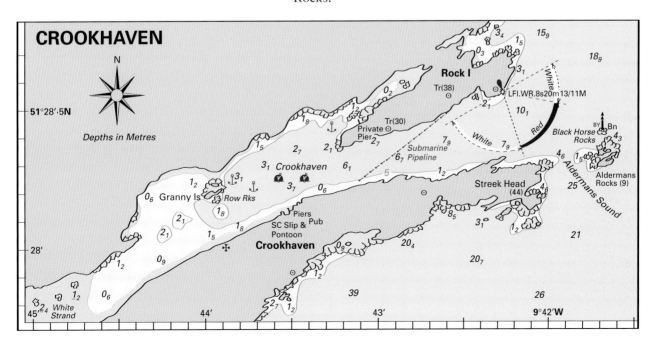

Brow Head

White Strand

The old pier for Rock Island

Road to Goleen

Crookhaven village and quays

Visitors' moorings

Rock Island lighthouse

End of public road

Crookhaven from NE

Dermot O'Sullivan runs the bar in his parents' pub and is extremely helpful with local knowledge. But do not ask him what the concrete structure on the north side of the harbour is – you will probably get an Irish reply to a FAQ. (It was actually for loading road-stone onto ships from the quarry above.)

Tenders completely monopolise Crookhaven's pontoon in high summer

CROOKHAVEN PILOTAGE

Tides HW Cóbh –0010

Crookhaven can be entered safely at any tide between the LH on Rock Island and the NCM on Black Horse Rocks, except with very strong easterlies. Night entrance is only for locals. There is no longer an anchorage in the channel south of Rock Island (submarine pipeline) but there are visitors' moorings just before the village. Many private moorings are haphazardly laid off the harbour but outside these there is plenty of room to anchor. Best shelter from easterlies is west of Granny Island or Rock Island.

BALLYDIVLIN AND TOORMORE BAYS

GOLEEN

Goleen is now best visited by road unless it is safe to anchor outside in deep water.

It has an excellent restaurant and is only 3km from a roadside quay on the north side of Crookhaven. Goleen's entrance has moorings for the fishing vessels, leaving little room to anchor. The renovated outer quay has good ladders where a yacht might get a berth alongside a fishing vessel. An inner quay dries but has a slip into deep water for tenders.

A walk on the wild side along the seaward coast of Crookhaven

GOLEEN PILOTAGE

Tides As Crookhaven

The entrance is a narrow cleft in the cliffs about 1 mile north of Crookhaven. Only one church can be seen now. Its green steeple on with a tall green cliff-edge pillar, bearing 276°, leads to the south side of the narrow entrance. Alternatively, align the spire with

Deserted Cornish miners' homes on Brow Head overlooking Barley Cove

Heron's Cove Restaurant

Long slip into deep water for tenders

Drying inner harbour

Moorings

Renovated outer quay

The tall green beacon throws a long shadow

Goleen looking E

Goleen's green steeple on with a tall green cliff-edge pillar, bearing 276°, leads to the south side of the narrow entrance

The megalithic wedge tomb in the bay leading into Toormore Cove

the south side of a rounded hill behind, letting the spire slide to the left approaching the coast. Houses are predominantly grey to the south and white to the north of the harbour. The end-on view of the grey quay shows in the entrance.

Dunmanus Harbour, Dunmanus Bay, with the high ground of Beara beyond the Sheep Peninsula

The megalithic wedge tomb outside Toormore Cove

Sheltered drying anchorage

Toormore Cove

Anchorage in 4m+

Toormore Bay anchorage looking NE

AROUND BALLYDIVLIN AND TOORMORE BAYS

Located in the far northwest corner of Toormore Bay is a sandy cove sheltered by Reenard (Point). Head in towards the rocks to the right of the small beach. Anchor in sand outside a few local moorings. The bay dries to abeam the wooded point to the north. Behind this is a larger beach where boats can dry out in almost complete shelter. Beyond the beaches are a few neat bungalows. On the eastern side of the adjacent bay (near car park on OSI 88) is a megalithic wedge tomb – a slab of rock on two uprights. This was used as an altar for saying mass, which was illegal in the Penal Times of the early 18th century. Toormore's pub is called Altar Inn and a nice conciliatory touch is that the Church of Ireland (Protestant) vicar lives at Altar Rectory. Land in the little inlet just north of Carrigmore.

CARRIGNASHOGGEE ANCHORAGE

The bay named Carrignashoggee north of Castle Point has a deep anchorage with swinging room inside a reef and off the small quay (shown on OSI) at approximately 51°29′.8N 09°37′.2W (do not use as a WP). *Balair* did not venture past the reef as the tide was too high.

Pier   Anchorage

The tide was too high for *Balair* to enter Carrignashoggee anchorage!

The castle on Castle Pont from Barrel Sound

Carrignashoggee
anchorage

Goat Island Little
daymark

Castle
Point

Lough Buidhe

Gun Point

Croagh Bay
anchorage

Looking W
towards
Crookhaven and
Goleen

The new quay at
Colla in Long
Island Channel

INTO THE CHANNELS FOR SCHULL

Tidal streams through the channels begin approx:
E-going HW Cóbh –0545
W-going HW Cóbh +0015
The strongest, at 1½kn, are in Long Island Channel

Keep the engine running to round Castle Point for Barrel Sound, inside Duharrig and Barrel Rocks. Motoring is the prudent way for a stranger to first negotiate such sounds. The castle has a natural moat – a bridged crevice in the rock. The tower's name (Leamcon) is said to mean 'hounds' leap', which is about the width of this gap. Keep in mid-channel now until Schull ('Skull'). Goat Island has a derelict cottage and Little Goat Island a white day mark for the safe passage through Man of War Sound. Long Island is still inhabited.

Numerous sheltered anchorages can be found in Long Island Channel. OSI 88 shows Colla has a new quay northwest of Coney Island at 51°30′.2N 09°34′.2W on the chart, with moorings and anchorage in 4m. Beware of underwater cable. Coola House Hotel, with a convivial bar and restaurant, is a short walk up the hill.

SCHULL

Schull is the pretty shopping town for the Mizen and should be included in a cruise. An excellent Spar supermarket has a car park with no height restriction and hardware shop stocking Calor, Kos and Gaz. Ice and laundry are no longer available from Barnett's – this is now a drapers. Spar sells ice and there is a laundrette in the main street. Petrol and green diesel are available from the car accessory, tool hire and internet shop!

The pier has a 'chippie' but for a fishing harbour rubbish disposal is non-existent. Fuchsia Books is the place to browse. Mary Mackie is very knowledgeable, on Ireland in particular, and will probably have the book you want. She sells local charts, too. There is a Planetarium at the Community College. For further information (there is no Tourist Office) visit Adele's Coffee Shop, pick up an area guide and buy her recipe book.

On Mount Gabriel, to west of the road at Barnacleeve Gap, there are Neolithic copper mines. Narrow horizontal shafts are hidden amongst the bracken. The ore was released by intense heat then hammering with stone mauls. There are 19th-century copper mines around Cosheen on the east side of the harbour, to the northeast of Rossbrin and on Horse Island. The ore was exported to Swansea from Cosheen Harbour, Rossbrin and Audley Cove.

SCHULL PILOTAGE

Tides HW Cóbh –0025

Strangers should not approach at night, but local boats use the powerful leading lights to enter from Long Island Bay. Tide is no problem but better shelter from southerlies is in Long Island Channel. Leave lit Bull Rock red beacon to port. The leading marks are conspicuous. There were no buoys marking the fairway in October; *Balair* just avoided the many pots and moorings. Street lights illuminate visitors' moorings east of the quay. It may be possible to berth alongside a fishing vessel at the quay. There is ice, water and usually a heron on the pier, which has a very good slip. Good holding was found off the new slip of very active Fastnet Marine Education Centre, 3 cables south of the pier. Land here for a shore-side footpath to town, but do not leave a tender on the slip. The pontoon at the main quay gets very

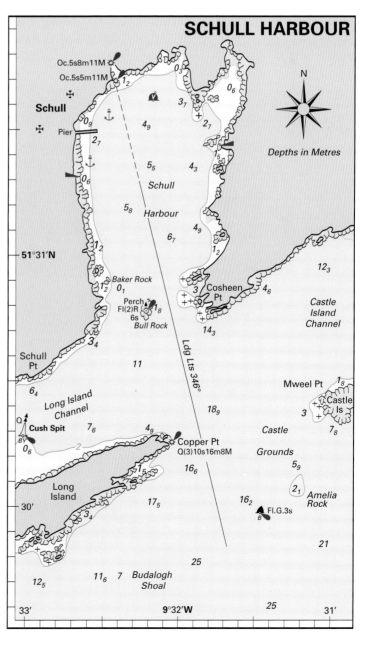

Visitors'
moorings

Pontoon for
tenders

Slip

Fastnet
Marine
Education
Centre's slip

Anchorage

**Schull Harbour
from SW**

**The lit red
beacon on Bull
Rock at the
entrance to
Schull**

**The pontoon at
Schull gets very
congested. An
Irish Naval
Service Vessel is
at anchor in the
outer harbour**

congested. For charts, chandlery and showers try Schull Water Sports Centre near the quay. Schull has held yacht races since the 19th century; the main event is 'Calves Week'. A marina is mooted.

CASTLE ISLAND ANCHORAGE

Departing from Schull, a lunch anchorage was taken in the bay on the south side of Castle Island. A spit extends further east across this bay than shown on the chart. This is just one of many similar DIY anchorages

amongst the islands between the Mizen and Baltimore. It has two beaches on an otherwise rocky foreshore. Ashore are the ruins of a castle and a few ruined cottages but only sheep now graze the deserted enclosures.

ROSSBRIN COVE

At HW *Balair* took Castle Spit and Horse Island Channel for Rossbrin Cove. This is a mud-hole at LW but it has a good boatyard. In the entrance, below the spectacular remains of a McCarthy castle, is an

From mussel farm in Roaringwater Bay towards Crookhaven

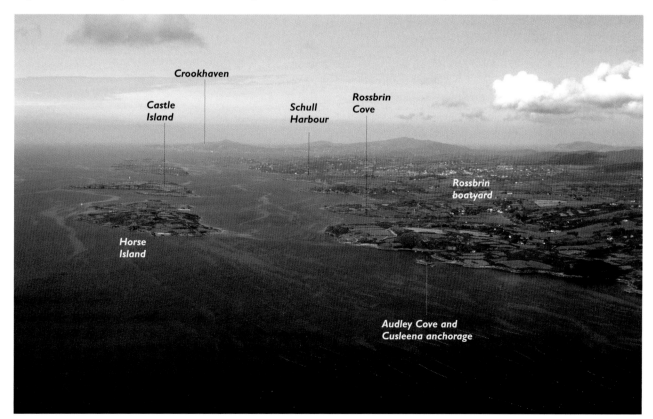

Looking downstream from Ballydehob
Cork Kerry Tourism

Final approach to Ballydehob's sandquay – seen at low water

Rock – marked by floating weed

Rock – marked by floating weed

Protruding steps

A dock, with a slip, on the N side of the quay

Walkway upstream of weir

Weir

Go alongside here

anchorage, but moorings leave little swinging room.

Use chart AC 2129 to escape from the cul-de-sac north of Horse Island. *Balair* was able to cross drying Horse Ridge for Roaringwater and Ballydehob Bays. A ferry serves modern homes on Horse Island.

Looking WNW from Roaringwater Bay over Kilcoe Castle, Poulgorm and Ballydehob Bays

CUSLEENA ANCHORAGE

Tucked in by the causeway to Cusleena Island there is an anchorage. Nearby Audley Cove once exported copper and slate, thus avoiding Horse Ridge. Ahead was *Balair*'s first sight of a major mussel farm, seemingly blocking the bays ahead from Rincolisky Castle on the mainland to actor Jeremy Irons' pastel pink Kilcoe Castle. Tom MacSweeney, in *Seascapes*, featured the sandboats which brought sea-sand into Ballydehob to enrich lime-deprived farm land. *Balair* just had to investigate. To reach Ballydehob Bay or the anchorage in Poulgorm Bay do not take the

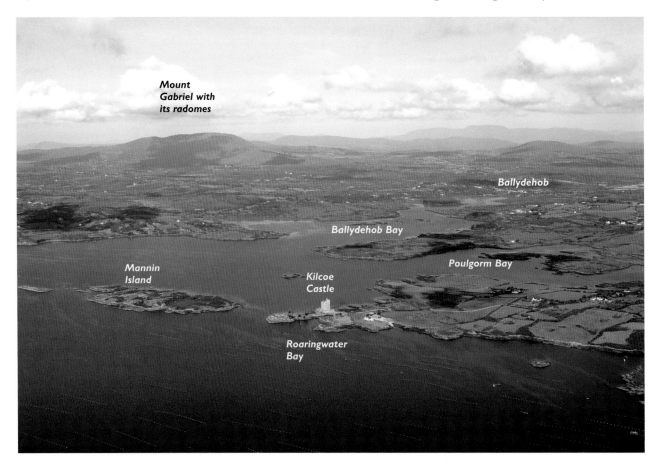

Mount Gabriel with its radomes

Ballydehob

Ballydehob Bay

Poulgorm Bay

Mannin Island

Kilcoe Castle

Roaringwater Bay

fairway shown on the chart or go between the rows of buoys; with wind or engine failure you could get entangled. (Take the cable-wide passage marked on the chart by the Mizen shore with 2m or more of water. But this is where crabbers set pots!)

BALLYDEHOB BAY

Tides HW as Schull

The water is so clear in Ballydehob Bay that any weed on the level bottom can be seen. Anchor off the quay shown on OSI 88. Landing by this quay, or on the south shore to explore or look at Audley and Rossbrin Coves, beware of mud and quicksands. The rocks above the anchorage mostly cover. To the northwest are the ever-visible floodlit domes on Mount Gabriel.

A trip by dinghy into Ballydehob is simple; on a rising tide it takes 20 minutes (by road it is 2½km). When past a tree-covered island, the arches of the old West Cork Railway bridge come into sight. This branch ran from Skibbereen to Schull, mainly for the fishing trade. The bridge is reflected in a lake below the town, created by a weir. Floating weed shows reefs on either side of the final approach to the well-preserved sand quay. A dock, with a slip, on the north side of the quay is used by small local boats. After inspection a yacht could dry out against the main (east) side of the quay, just above protruding steps. The bottom is firm with small stones. Schooners and sandboats did this regularly; had weather and season not beckoned *Balair* would have done so too.

Erik Haugard, Danish sailor and writer, lives in the old stores on the quay. He could not recall a visiting yacht. 300m from the quay is a water tap, then bottle bank and litter bins. Further on are tennis and basketball courts. The town has a golf range with a five-hole course. A service station has groceries, as does a small shop up the main street. There is a laundrette and hardware, health and gourmet food stores and a good second-hand bookshop. One pub displays a quote from James Joyce's *Ulysses*: 'A good puzzle would be to cross Ireland without passing a pub'. Do not pass Levis' Sandboat, where photographs of sandboats and other sailing craft grace the walls. Mrs Levis is the widow of one of the last sandboat skippers. Her son Cormac, school master, nautical historian and member of the Ilen River Sailing Club, has written *Almost Forgotten Harbours,* available at the bar.

The pub not to pass in Ballydehob!

POULGORM BAY

This adjoining bay was visited briefly. Overlooked by Kilcoe Castle, with another natural moat, this is a less sheltered anchorage with (in 2003) a noisy 'quarry'. Unfortunately this sound pervades many otherwise peaceful anchorages. Slate is easily split to face the many concrete-block homes that are being thrown up everywhere in Ivernia. Both bays and the river up to Ballydehob have lovely spots for picnics.

**Cattle graze the Mizen shore in Roaringwater Bay.
The Mizen is the whole peninsula**

**The white chapel, used in a clearing transit, is just
below the ridge with green fields below – westward
of a small mound west of the highest point of Clear.
Taken looking down the transit of 190°**

Chapel

THROUGH THE ISLANDS OF
LONG ISLAND BAY

Leaving Ballydehob the Mizen shore has two quays between Foilnamuch and Knockrower Points. These are private as they front large houses with well kept lawns. (Much lawn-mowing takes place throughout Cork and Kerry.) Looking down the channels from Horse Island to Brow Head, Crookhaven's entrance is just obscured.

For passages through the reefs and islands of Long Island Bay use the charts and pilots; in fine weather these make for interesting pilotage. Unless the wind is free the stranger is advised to motor. Under power Carthy Sound needs no clearing line to avoid Moore's Rock; just keep close to Horse and Castle Islands.

Between Baltimore and the Mizen peninsula it is easiest to route just east of Calf Island East or keep east of the Calf Islands. Mount Gabriel's domes and Barnacleave Gap are excellent marks to the north. South-bound, unless the white chapel on Cape Clear Island can be seen, the clearing transit of 190° between Rowmore reef and Moore's Rock to clear Anima Rock is useless. Until close to Clear it is impossible to pick out Illauneana against the coast. The chapel is on high ground with green fields below, westward of a small mound west of the highest point of Clear. Many of the dangers will show their presence with breakers.

This is the place to browse, find the book you want or purchase a chart in Schull

Mizen Head. When *Balair* returns she will have rounded Mizen Head for Dunmanus and Bantry Bays

3 MIZEN HEAD TO DURSEY HEAD

Adrigole Harbour in Bantry Bay
overlooked by Hungry Hill, looking W
towards Bear Haven

3 MIZEN HEAD TO DURSEY HEAD

Ports, harbours and anchorages

Dunmanus Bay
Dunmanus Harbour – Dunbeacon Cove – Dunbeacon Harbour
Kitchen Cove (Ahakista) – Anchorages on southern shore of Sheep's Head

Bantry Bay
Bantry Harbour – Glengarriff Adrigole Harbour – Trafrask Bay – Lonehort Harbour – Dunboy Bay
Bearhaven – Mill Cove – Lawrence Cove Marina
Pulleen Harbour – Black Ball Harbour

Arrival port
Castletownbere

Charts and maps
Passage and planning charts
  Imray C56, AC 2424
Essential large-scale charts
  AC 2552, 1840, 1838, 2184, 2495
OSI Discovery Series maps 88, 85, 84

Coastguard radio relay stations with working channels
Mizen Head Ch 04
Bantry Ch 23

RNLI Lifeboats
Castletownbere

Important landfall lights
Fastnet Rock
Mizen Head
Sheep's Head
The Bull
Ardnarkinna Point

Differential GPS Station
Mizen Head

Tourist Information
Cork Kerry Tourism, Aras Fáilte, Grand Parade, Cork
☎ 021 4273251 *Fax* 021 4273504
Email info@corkkerrytourism.ie
www.ireland.travel.ie

Local Tourist Information
Beara Tourism & Development Association
☎/*Fax* 027 70054
Email bearatours@eircom.net
www.bearatourism.com
Bantry Tourism Association
☎ 027 50229
www.westcork.com/bantry-tourism

A BRIEF DESCRIPTION OF THE AREA

Most of the cruising is in Bantry Bay. Just around Mizen Head narrow Dunmanus Bay lies between sparsely inhabited shores, with two unspoilt natural harbours and lagoon-like Dunbeacon Harbour. This has good anchorages, or an alongside berth, within easy reach of shops and pubs in attractive Durrus village at the tidal mouth of Four Mile Water.

Sheep's Head, also known as Muntervary, is the narrow finger of West Cork which separates Dunmanus and Bantry Bays. It is an easy day sail from Kitchen Cove, on Muntervary's south shore, to Castletownbere, Bantry Harbour or Glengarriff. Bantry, protected from the west by Whiddy Island, has several good anchorages, visitors' moorings, a possible alongside berth and excellent shops. Bantry House should not be missed.

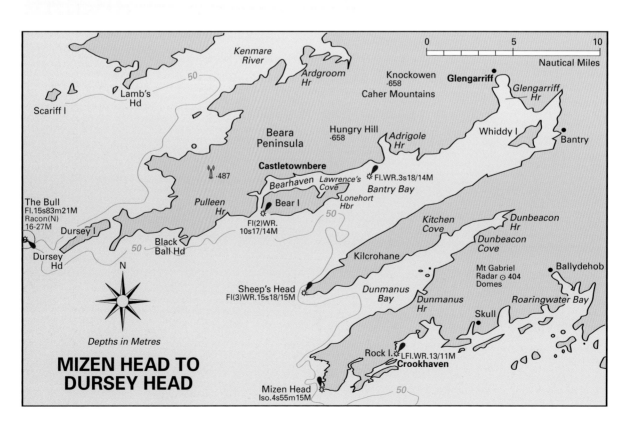

MIZEN HEAD TO DURSEY HEAD

Fortified Whiddy has a good anchorage and interesting walks from the ferry pier, where there is a pub. Just north of Whiddy is beautiful Glengarriff Harbour, with visitors' moorings and plenty of anchorages. Ashore is for the tourist but the gardens created on once-rocky Illinacullen (Garinish Island) should be visited. The Beara forms the north shore of Bantry Bay and the only natural harbours worth visiting between Glengarriff and Bearhaven are Trafrask Bay and Adrigole, a large inlet lying under foreboding Hungry Hill. Between Bear Island and Dursey there are just two small inlets to visit – but only in settled weather.

CASTLETOWNBERE

Castletownbere (CTB for brevity), on the south side of the Beara peninsula, is one of the Republic's most important fishing ports. Castletown was the English name when Bear Haven was, with Cóbh and Crookhaven, an important anchorage for the Atlantic Fleet. These anchorages were retained by Britain after the Treaty of 1922 until 1938. Near the western end of Bantry Bay, Castletownbere is an ideal arrival and victualling port with nearby Lawrence Cove Marina, Bear Island, for alongside diesel and water. Green diesel is available, by can, from CTB's Co-op on Dinish Island. Fish ice is also available from Dinish.

CTB has hostels offering showers. Pubs and restaurants are excellent. The one main

Standing stone near Castletownbere (shown on OSI 84)

street continues along the sea front. There are many butchers but only one fish shop; the Irish prefer to export their catch to France and Spain! A new hotel which would suit an awaiting crew overlooks the harbour. There is a small chandler. Gaz is available from a good hardware/builders' merchant and from SuperValu.

Beara Tourism, in the square, has much information on the whole of the Beara peninsula and also has an excellent website (see previous page). The leaflet *Ring of Beara* has a good map of the peninsula giving all the facilities on its Bantry Bay and Kenmare River shores. The full history of Bantry Bay is well told at Call of the Sea, a visitor centre up the road past SuperValu. This, along with *A Bay of Destiny* by Michael Carol, will explain why Bantry Bay has so many fortifications.

Castletownbere Harbour from SE

Dinish Island   Irish Coastguard depot   Visitors' moorings

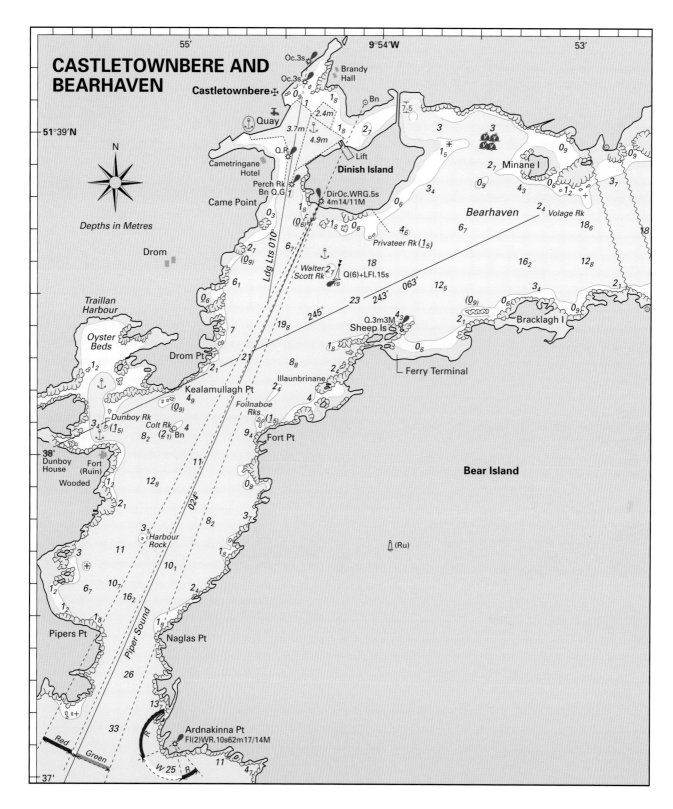

CASTLETOWNBERE AND BEARHAVEN

(For exploring, use *Beara – A Journey through History* by Daniel O'Brien, noting that he calls walls between fields 'fences'.) Using the straight old main road to the copper mining village of Eyeries, the standing stones shown on OSI 84 are easy to find. There are longer excursions along the Beara Way. The copper mines, fictionalised by Daphne du Maurier in *Hungry Hill*, were on the Kenmare River coast of Beara but are tricky to visit from a boat. MacCarthy's

Grocery and Bar is the place to meet local people. Adrienne MacCarthy took over from Dr Aidan MacCarthy, whose traumatic experiences as a Japanese POW are on display. Adrienne is also a voluntary member of the Irish Coast Guard, who have one of their large land stations on Dinish Island. Before departing for Lawrence Cove Marina energetic crew could ferry across to Bear Island and rejoin ship after a 6km hike across the island.

CASTLETOWNBERE PILOTAGE

Tides HW Cóbh −0030
RNLI Offshore Severn

There is adequate water for a yacht, on the leading lines, through the narrow main west entrance (Piper Sound) between Bear Island and the mainland and then into the harbour. This approach can be used at any tide and at night. A strong southwesterly against the ebb can make it uncomfortable. The entrance is marked by Ardnakinna lighthouse. With this abeam the large red leading marks (the front has a directional light) on 024° are easily picked up by day. There is a wider eastern entrance, only to be used by day as it is encumbered by mid-channel rocks, uncharted marine farms and a wrecked merchantman with masts still showing! These hazards are lit but local knowledge is required at night. Either entrance is beautiful. Slieve Miskish and Hungry Hill rise to the north, often into cumulus – sometimes in mizzle.

When intercepting the final 010° leading line into harbour, marked by red and white striped leading marks (with lights), look out for the frequent Bear Island ferry. This passes Walter Scott SCM on NNW and SSE tracks. The final approach for all craft is between the green pillar on Perch Rock and a red pillar further in; they have Q.G and Q.R lights.

Entering Castletownbere with Perch Rock SHM ahead. Inner leading marks (vertical red stripe on white) to left of Perch Rock. Red and white ferry is at its slip with red piles. Anchorage is to starboard outside lifeboat

Bear Haven from Bear Island
Joy Swanson

From the anchorage in Castletownbere harbour with the large white Irish Coast Guard station on Dinish Island beyond the lifeboat

Castletownbere is a major fishing harbour with no facilities for yachts, though they are welcome to anchor

After Perch Rock turn starboard for the anchorage between the lifeboat and the quays on Dinish Island. Leave room for trawlers and the Bear Island ferry which berths at the slip (with red piles) near SuperValu. Shore lighting is sufficient for anchoring. In high summer yachts frequently anchor too close for comfort! By arrangement with a fishing vessel a yacht can occasionally raft up just to the northeast of CTB's trawler quays. There are good steps here, and skips which open just enough for galley waste. The harbour is sheltered by Dinish Island, which has recently been developed as a further major facility for the fishing fleet. The harbourmaster is friendly but is adamant that his harbour is for very large fishing vessels and has absolutely no facilities for yachts, though they are very welcome to anchor. There are rather remote visitors' moorings, which do not get much use, to the east, between Dinish and Minane Islands.

DUNMANUS BAY

Tides Use HW Castletownbere

Coasting from Crookhaven to round Mizen Head, the most southwesterly point of mainland Ireland, Brow Head has an old signal tower and the ruins of one of Marconi's coastal radio stations. After the tower there is a mine engine-house perched, like many in Cornwall, halfway down to the sea. Barley Cove has lovely strands and looks a tempting anchorage, but only in very settled weather. Buried under the sands are the bodies of many seamen from French vessels wrecked after the unsuccessful armada of 1796 into Bantry Bay, intended to free Ireland from English rule. (See Michael Carol's *A Bay of Destiny*.)

Approaching Mizen head beware of Carrignagower, over a cable from the coast. Keep outside its breakers! The coast has been gouged, very like that of Cape Clear, by Atlantic storms. Mizen Head is a relatively low extension of much higher Mizen Peak, and though it now shows just a light it was primarily a signal (wireless telegraphy) and fog warning station. It has a DGPS station and is separated from the mainland by a rocky gorge spanned by an arched concrete bridge. Under this lies the wreck of a French frigate retreating from Bantry; many cannonballs still litter the bottom. Ironically, she was driven ashore by a southwest gale after being blown out of Bantry Bay by an easterly. Just to the east there is now an excellent Visitor Centre, accessed by road from Crookhaven or Schull, with much of interest to sailors.

A relatively shallow spit extends from the point. Northbound, in benign sea and wind conditions, *Balair* passed inside the 3.8m sounding. The worst of any overfalls can usually be avoided by staying just outside in 20m, but Mizen Head is not to be trifled with. From the north the remains of an old cable bridge are visible. A similar but longer reef extends off Three Castle Head. The passage inside South Bullig was taken northbound. Many diving sea birds work this reef, as they do other shallows. Close in there is just one old castle; from an offing the stumps of the others are visible.

Sinuous Dursey Island and the rounded hills west of Castletownbere open up beyond this headland, then Sheep's Head just 3½ miles away.

The westernmost coasts of Dunmanus Bay have few habitations. Its southern shores, being protected from most gales, are not as rugged as those to the north. Coasting up the south shore a very green and pointed island lies just off the coast. Bird Island is where puffins and shearwaters make their nesting burrows. Pleasant features of this unspoilt scrubby coast are the green cols with sheep, and maybe a few cattle and a solitary farmhouse. The coast road, meandering as once did the goat, is almost completely hidden.

DUNMANUS HARBOUR

Tides HW Cóbh –0050

Proceeding eastwards, sheltered Dunmanus Harbour is the first haven on this shore. The conspicuous castle first shows over low Dunmanus Point. The numerous rocks which reduce the cable-wide entrance appreciably and the castle are shown on the chart. Keeping the castle on 173° will bring you nicely in to drop anchor in 4–5m, just outside local moorings. With the furze ablaze, this is still, to quote ISDs, 'a wild and attractive place'. Mussels and other shellfish abound. On the western shores several sheltered sandy coves are ideal for cooking these. New houses are being built here as there is now a nearby main road. Going ashore you will encounter the long and profuse weed which the clear, clean and warm waters north of the Mizen produce. One often needs to row the last ten yards or so into a landing place.

Behind Rinneen Island there is a small quay, in frequent used by fishing vessels. By

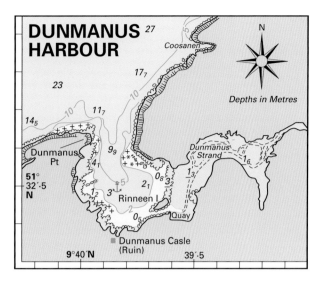

arrangement, a medium-size boat can dry out against the eastern wall. Water is available from nearby houses but there are no nearby stores. It is only a 7km round walk to the shop in Toormore in Long Island Bay. Visit the megalithic tomb and return via Toormore Bay anchorage and wild country roads.

DUNBEACON COVE

Tides HW Cóbh –0040

With good visibility and weather the passage eastwards between Carbery and Furze Islands, then between Cold Island and

Dunmanus Harbour from N

Murphy rocks, is straightforward. An Englishman has a modern home behind Brandy Point on Carbery, with natural and diesel generators, a deep well, a floating pontoon, boat and small beach. His nearest neighbours are the seals. To the northeast the conspicuous chapel above Kitchen Cove, on the Sheep, was yellow in 2004.

Dunbeacon Cove is where Dunmanus Bay narrows to a river estuary. This very narrow inlet is only suitable for a boat of 8m or less. Seen from the west the remains of the castle look like a leaning tower, with a small wooded hill to the right and a white dwelling on either side. There is no large-scale plan but entrance to this very small creek is straight forward at LW with all reefs showing. Come in on 144° towards the large yellow (2004) house, with Mount Gabriel's spheres above. On 25m of chain in 3m on clean sand, *Balair* swung with 50 yards to spare from the rocks on either side alongside the castle. This was a planned night stop before shopping in Durrus in the morning. Had it not been dead calm a better anchorage would have been just outside the cove. The quay is not visible when at anchor. It must dry, so a better landing is on the steep gravel beach near the main road. Provided you are happy to leave a boat at anchor, there is a well-preserved stone circle on the western slopes of Mount Corrin.

Return by the main road to collect a loaf and a bottle of milk from the Dunbeacon Campsite shown on OSI 88. This is in a pleasant garden setting and welcomes motor caravans.

DUNBEACON HARBOUR

Tides HW Cóbh –0040

Departing from pretty Dunbeacon Cove there are all the signs of an ancient estuary, with shores and elongated islands of loose alluvial soil and vegetation to match. The marks for the 078° leading line into Dunbeacon Harbour have been deleted on the chart but this track avoids the shallows and rocks on the Mizen side. The southern part of the harbour has a large mussel farm, easily avoided – as is Carrigbroanty – on a track of 045° from close Mannion's Island towards a conspicuous new quay at the entrance to Four Mile Water. Fishing vessels berth mainly on the upstream side of the quay and there is a good slip. There is about 2m on the outside of the quay with good ladders and tyings, suitable for a high water shopping trip. (The harbour is not so deep.) At HW neaps –0300 there is plenty of water beyond the quay as far as an old grain warehouse. *Balair* anchored further on in 0.5m, opposite the first house on the north bank and about ¼ mile below the derelict quay shown on the plan. This is covered with brambles and furze. Just below it is a shingle landing place about a 15-minute walk from Durrus village. Do not try to get closer by tender because of profuse weed.

Food shopping is sufficient; one store takes Visa and dispenses diesel and petrol. There is a small repair garage, good hardware, post office, ladies' hairdresser and, of course, pubs. The free *Sheep's Head Way Map* lists all the facilities in the peninsula. Riverside Gardens, with an old mill leat full of trout, are worth the small entrance fee. The river is now rocky and gets a run of sea-trout and salmon. The owners kindly let the author browse without charge and gave him coffee and biscuits.

In the lagoon-like outer harbour there are plenty of safe neap tide anchorages clear of the mussel farm. OSI 88 suggests interesting walks with easy access to the Sheep's Head Way or the stone circle on the slopes of bosom-like Mount Corrin. The pier to the north side is also derelict but there are plenty of gravel landing beaches.

Top
Heading into Dunbeacon Cove with domes on Mt Gabriel over yellow house

Bottom
From anchorage in Dunbeacon Cove

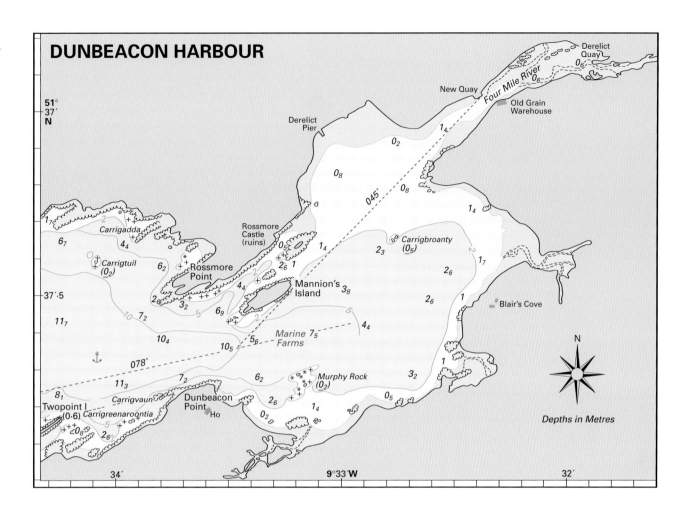

DUNBEACON HARBOUR

51° 37′ N

Derelict Quay

0·6′

New Quay

Four Mile River

0·6

Old Grain Warehouse

Derelict Pier

0·2

1·4

0·8

0·8

045°

1·4

Carrigbroanty (0·6)

1·4

Rossmore Castle (ruins)

0·5

1·4

2·3

1·7

37′·5

1·7

2

Carrigadda

6·7

4·4

Carrigtuil (0·2)

6·2

Rossmore Point

4·4

2·6 1

Mannion's Island 3·8

2·6

2·6

2·6

1

Blair's Cove

2·6

3·2

6·9

2

5

4·4

11·7

10

7·2

10·4

10·5

5·6

Marine 7·5 Farms

078°

11·3

7·2

6·2

Murphy Rock (0·2)

3·2

1

8·1

Carrigvaun

Dunbeacon Point

2·6

1·4

0·5

Twopoint I (0·6) Carrigreenaroontia

Ho

0·2

0·8

2·6

N

Depths in Metres

34′   9°33′W   32′

Dunmanus Bay. Dunbeacon Harbour from SW

Durrus

New Quay

Derelict pier

Mussel farm

New quay at entrance to Four Mile Water,
Dunbeacon Harbour, from anchorage above

New pier at Ahakista (Kitchen Cove) looking NE

KITCHEN COVE (AHAKISTA)

Tides HW Cóbh –0040

From Dunbeacon Harbour it is an interesting short passage to Kitchen Cove. Round the reef extending southwest from Owen's Island in 10m and come in on a steady bearing to Ahakista's new concrete pier. This will clear the dangerous drying rock 1.75 cables southwest of the pier. (This is unofficially marked with a red flag!) The cove is full of small-boat moorings but anchored a cable south-southwest of the quay the views are beautiful. Ahakista House nestles amongst the many trees which thrive in the alluvial soil. Your boat can be seen from the beer garden by the quay. Paddy and Mary have been landlords for 37 years so the unspoilt Arundel deserves a mention. It is used mainly

Dunmanus Bay. Kitchen Cove from W

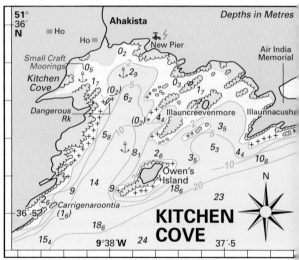

by locals, including a former TD (Member of Parliament) whose wife sings sea shanties.

A few fishing vessels use the quay which has water, AC and room for a yacht to dry out near the shore. Ahakista has another pub, a basic store, a house selling wine and a post box, all well scattered. There are plenty of good walks, one up and over the long spine of the Sheep for views over Bantry Bay. There were many vapour trails overhead as Ahakista is near one of the reporting points where transatlantic aircraft change between Shannon's HF Oceanic and VHF Terrestrial Control. In June 1985 Air India Flight 182 from Canada was destroyed by a bomb near Sheep's Head. 329 souls perished. This explains the lovely memorial garden on nearby Illaunacusha.

FAIR-WEATHER ANCHORAGES ON MUNTERVARY'S SOUTHERN SHORES

There are temporary anchorages further west on the Sheep. Both are sheltered from northwesterlies. That east of Kilcrohane Point has a nice landing pier, a shingle beach and is 1km from Kilcrohane. This is the largest village in Muntervary, with shops, a traditional pub, restaurant, petrol and diesel. On Fridays there is a butter market. 1½miles west there is another anchorage off the old

Pier at Kilcrohane looking **NE**

Dunmanus Bay, Kilcrohane looking **W**

Sheep's Head

Anchorage off Trawgroom

Sandy cove facing southwest, by Sheep's Head Way leading to Kilcrohane

Old steamer quay northeast of Dooneen Point

Kilcrohane pier

Small craft moorings

steamer quay northeast of Dooneen Point, with a turning bollard on a nearby rock. It is a wild place. The pier has steps but is only suitable for a dinghy. 7 cables to the east, however, a small sandy cove faces southwest, by the Sheep's Head Way leading to Kilcrohane. (This was not investigated closely.) A mile west of Dooneen Point is an interesting-looking anchorage off Trawgrooim with a pier and beach by the Sheep's Head Way. It would be an 8-mile hike to the lighthouse, where I saw a family of young choughs fluttering and chirping around the rocks. Off-road, the Way can be tough going!

Those fortunate enough to be cruising Dunmanus Bay in settled weather, and who like discovering interesting day anchorages and walking, will find this central southern coast of the Sheep fascinating, with good sheltered night anchorages in nearby Dunmanus or Ahakista. Landings can also be made on Furze and Carbery Islands.

The rest of this coast is again wild and beautiful, with little habitation; but this was not always so. In places the steep mountainside has old stone enclosures right to the clifftops. These are from Celtic times, not those of the Great Famine. West Cornwall, north of Land's End, has identical fields. Atlantic storms have taken their toll on these cliffs, causing many landslides.

Having passed a cluster of 19th-century houses – probably for the old coastguard – look for the word Eire picked out in white stones. This was no doubt to remind the Royal Navy, as they entered Bantry Bay, that they were now in the waters of a Free State. If anything, Sheep's Head looks – from the south – more like that of an alligator, complete with eye! It has another Bullig Reef,

EIRE in white stones on south side of Sheep's Head

but the inside passage in 15m was smooth half an hour before HW. For both Dunmanus and Bantry Bays treat each ria as a large estuary, with streams flooding and ebbing.

BANTRY BAY

Tides Use HW Castletownbere

SHEEP'S HEAD TO BANTRY

For the visitor it is now more practical to make the six-mile crossing to Castletownbere from Sheep's Head, as there are no havens on the south shore before Bantry.

The north coast of the Sheep is wild like that of the Mizen until approaching Whiddy Island. Whilst admiring the grandeur of the Slieves and Mountains of the Beara (only

Sheep's Head looks, from the south, more like that of an alligator – complete with eye!

some seven miles to the north), keep an eye out for several coastal marine farms, starting at about 09°42′W. These are worked out of a tiny harbour in Loughaun, inside League Point. There are two more well offshore, over a shoal patch at 09°36′W marked by Indigo NCM. This is the first of three SHMs for the deep-water channel to Whiddy oil terminal; with two PHMs off the northern shore of Bantry Bay. In January 1979 a fire destroyed the tanker *Betelgeuse* and the offshore terminal was closed. This has been replaced by a large SPM 8 cables NNW of Whiddy connected by floating hoses to the island. Give this a berth of at least 530m if heading for Glengarriff. There is a historic wreck just north of the SPM, part of the unsuccessful armada.

BANTRY HARBOUR PILOTAGE

SOUTH ENTRANCE
(Only for small craft in fair weather)

Tides HW Cóbh –0035
Tidal streams up to 1½kn

We now enter the old estuary of the Coomhala River, which ran through Bantry Harbour, leaving a great shingle bank (Whiddy) to the north and the alluvial mound of Blue Hill to the south, with small islands and shingle banks in the harbour. Michael Carol explains all this in his *A Bay of*

Destiny. Ahead is the shallow south entrance to Bantry, the shortest route from the west but not to be attempted in rough conditions. Streams there can reach 1½kn. AC 1838 is essential for this entrance. The leading marks no longer exist. Approaching Relane Point establish on 063° as shown on the chart, between the point and Cracker Rock. This aligns with the seaward edge of the airfield, marked by red and white striped posts, with distant Reenbeg Head, a rounded hill. A bearing on the poles gives sufficient guidance, leaving the man-made escarpment of Blue Hill to starboard. In late summer beware of shrimp pots on long and possibly floating lines supported by makeshift buoys. These are a hazard throughout southwest Ireland at this season.

In late afternoon on a sunny day the view of the rounded cloud-capped mountains beyond Bantry – itself nestling between low green hills – is stunning. The best anchorage for visiting this market town is northwest of Bantry House, 2–3 cables from the pier, east of small craft, visitors' and sailing club moorings.

Beware of the old ballast bank (2.3m) close to the shore below the house. Trading vessels once moored or came alongside here at Black Rock, where there is a disused swimming platform. Small yachts can dry out against the inside of Bantry pier near the shore. There is a handy ladder. The northern part of Bantry

Bantry harbour from W

Reenbeg Point

Disused railway and steamer pier

Black Rock

Bantry Bay Sailing Club and slip

Burial ground on site of 15th-century Franciscan Abbey

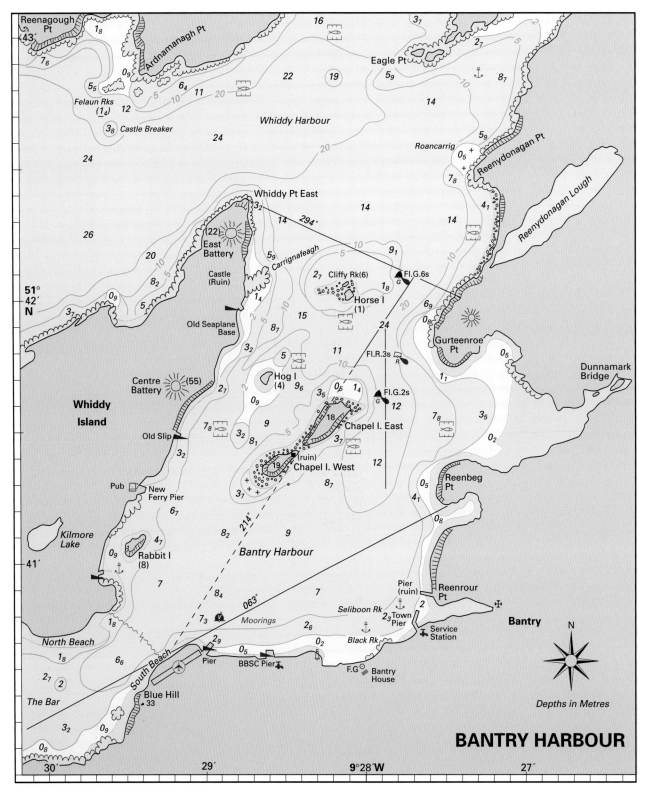

BANTRY HARBOUR

Depths in Metres

harbour is a mass of mussel farms, their boats cluttering Bantry pier which is also used by Whiddy ferries. The ferries make a bad (but infrequent) wash in the anchorage.

Bantry House has a valuable collection of furniture and tapestries, much of it collected in France after the Revolution. In a stable-yard there is a museum dedicated to the French Armada of 1796. The 18th-century house hosts an annual Music Festival. To visit use the first small pier, with a slip, off the moorings in front of the yacht club. Mussel

boats have taken over the other pier to the west. Secure the tender by the side ladder as club boats go alongside to slip or for water. The club has showers and free moorings for visitors with a contact number displayed. To the west is a burial ground where a Franciscan abbey stood in 1462. There is a tall granite cross in memory of the 51 people who perished in the *Betelgeuse* fire. On a plaque are the words: 'Here lie the victims whose names are known only to God alone'. Continue up the main road and turn left past

The entrance of Bantry House

West Lodge Hotel; in about 1km look for the sign for the Kilurane Pillar Stone above the road. This has interesting carvings and there are good views over Bantry Harbour.

BANTRY TOWN

Until settled by the English in 1600 this was a fishing hamlet on a small creek. With this new wealth, fishing became a major industry – as was wool – and a trading port was established. It is now a very attractive and important centre of commerce for West Cork. The upper part of the creek has long been built over and an attractive new square, dedicated to the lawyer Wolfe Tone (who led the unsuccessful French Armada) fronts the drying old harbour. There is an excellent tourist office in the old Court House. The *Heritage Guide to Bantry Town* and all the other information available will guide you, as does the excellent website www.westcork.com/bantry-tourism

With an express bus service from Cork, Bantry is very convenient for joining crews. There are many good shops and a SuperValu. Green diesel is available from the Bantry Tyre Company or GW Biggs, but suitable transport is needed. Contact the friendly sailing club for this. There is a service station selling road diesel by the harbour. Camping Gaz is available in the town.

Self-drive car hire

See *Appendix*

WHIDDY ISLAND

There is a peaceful sheltered anchorage southwest of Rabbit Island, just off the private slip of an attractive farmhouse. Unfortunately many mussel boats clutter the other anchorages along this shore. You can anchor south of the new ferry pier, where there is a good pub with food and tennis. An old slip near the Central battery is convenient for exploring on foot. The remains of a First World War American seaplane base (used for submarine spotting), a ruined castle and another Battery are further north. The three batteries on Whiddy are really redoubts developed in the early 19th century against further French incursions. They were built on the defences of the O'Sullivans, who once ruled most of Bantry Bay.

BANTRY HARBOUR PILOTAGE

NORTH ENTRANCE

Tides HW Cóbh –0035
VHF HM Ch 14, others Ch 11
Tides slack

Entering Bantry by the southern entrance. Established on 263° with the seaward edge of the airfield (marked with red and white striped poles) on with distant Reenbeg Head

The old drying harbour below Bantry

The deep-water channel is lit as far as the Oil Terminal's SPM. For the mussel boats, which work at night, there are buoys with lights marking the north entrance to Bantry Harbour. Without local knowledge yachts should not attempt a night arrival. Fish farms, which will be lit, surround this approach but they are very much a movable feast! The Harbour Commissioners, who make regular surveys, ensure that no new ones encroach on the shipping channels. There is plenty of water all the way to the pier and anchorages. (The disused pier was the terminal of the West Cork Railway.) A sheltered anchorage can always be found; these are shown on the plan. Do not anchor by the 8.4m sounding; this is on the track of the Whiddy ferries. There is another just inside the estuary of the Coomhola River, outside the harbour – in the northeast corner of the chart.

It is possible to enter between Whiddy and Horse Island, but the buoyed channel is the one recommended. The buoys are large and easy to pick out. Keep Whiddy Point East on 294° astern to clear shallows north of Horse Island, then go around the first SHM just past the island. The course is now 214° with the escarpment on Blue Hill seen between the Chapel Islands. When Horse Island bears northwest proceed south between the PHM off Gurteenroe Point and the SHM northeast of Chapel Island East. All these islands, including Whiddy, are drumlins – elongated

ridges of silt and gravel left in this once-great river estuary.

The Harbour Commissioners' excellent website (www.bantrybayport.com) is written for craft large and small. Just click on 'Shipman Ltd'.

Wofe Tone's statue in the new square at Bantry

GLENGARRIFF

Tides HW Cóbh –0035

Yachts visit this lovely natural harbour for its beauty and the subtropical gardens on Illnacullen. The village is overrun by tourists in the summer. It has limited shopping, road fuel and Kos. Eccles Hotel offers showers for sailors. Before 0900 and after 1800 it is possible to get alongside the pleasure ferry berth on the main pier to top up with water.

See the guide books for interesting walks around the valley of the Glengarriff River, which still retains ancient woodland. Illnacullen was bare but for the Martello tower and scrub until sold by the British War Office in 1910. The private owners imported soil, stone and plants to create the unique gardens of today.

Balair found pilotage into Glengarriff, between the rocks off Ship Island and the eastern shore, straightforward; keeping well to starboard in the narrows. Just before these is a mussel farm with another in the bay off the castle. The latter is mainly concealed by trees. Many new 'white houses' postdate those on the chart, but the one (with tall chimneys) by the harbour is still a useful mark. (Refer to ISDs for fuller guidance.) Mussel boats and passenger ferries make it difficult to berth at the pier. A new dinghy pier is located nearer the hotel. There are visitors' moorings and ample room to anchor in mud clear of dangers. A good anchorage is just north of Bark Island. To visit Illnacullen

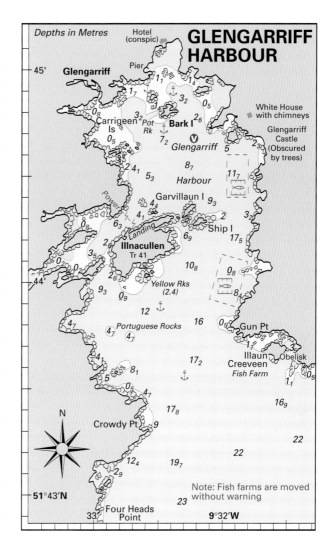

Glengarriff Harbour from SE

Bark Island, Glengarriff Harbour, on a misty morning in May

anchor near Otter Island and land at the slip on the northwest side. Ferries berth to the right of this, so tie up on the other side. There is a beach here but the only access to the island is via the slip. The gardens and exotic trees are well described in a booklet available at the turnstile. Visit early, before the constant visitors arrive by ferry. The coffee shop is excellent. Return south-about to see many 'tame' seals on the rocks. An excellent touring caravan site is at Eagle Point, midway between Glengarriff and Bantry.

Illnacullen, Glengarriff Harbour

Martello Tower on once fortified Illnacullen, protecting Glengarriff Harbour

PROCEEDING WESTWARDS FROM GLENGARRIFF

Departing from Glengarriff in favourable conditions it is safe to pass close to Four Heads Point in 20m, then to route inside Coulagh Rocks PHM and between Sheelane Island and Garinish West. Otherwise keep outside the PHMs for big ships.

This north coast of Bantry Bay has two other anchorages before Bear Island. The woods soon give way to the most rugged mountains seen so far, much grooved by the departing ice. Sugarloaf Mountain is well named. Britain's Astronomer Royal, Sir Patrick Moore, has a simple holiday home on Garinish with views over most of Bantry Bay. Sheelane has a stone day mark. Ahead, a large vessel may be moored close in to the east of Leahill Point, collecting stone from a cliff-side quarry. Further on, Cromwell landed for his march to overthrow O'Sullivan Bere at Dunboy Castle in 1602. Shot Head conceals southwest-facing Trafrask Bay. This has one visitors' mooring off a quay, small local boats, a few cottages, a shop and a pub serving food. A good round walk is up the river valley taking in part of the Beara Way, with several antiquities on route. This mountain stream should have good trouting where it backs up behind the beach.

ADRIGOLE HARBOUR

Tides HW Cóbh –0030

Adrigole's lovely harbour with stark Hungry Hill (which lent its name to Daphne du Maurier's copper mining saga) rising beyond is still one of the few true natural harbours in Southwest Ireland – it is not sheltered by islands.

At Shot Head set course to clear the rock awash at chart datum before Adrigole. Soil left by ice and an ancient river, which must also have scoured out Bearhaven, has created a low-lying fertile coastal strip. Off to port is Roancarrigmore lighthouse, guarding the rocky entrance to Bearhaven. A bearing on the white chapel, partly concealed by trees, at Drumlave serves to clear the dangerous rock. Leave the mussel farm inside the harbour entrance, the rocks and Orthon's Island to port. Anchor near a raft used by the sailing school, just northwest of the pier. There are also visitors' moorings. Seals may be drying out on rocks beyond Orthon's Island. There is better shelter from strong gusts, from the mountains, off Reen Lodge (see plan) but first negotiate this area at LW to ensure swinging room from rocks. Land near Reen Bridge to view the spectacular waterfall on Hungry

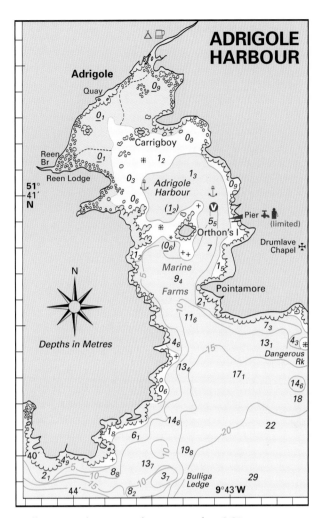

Hill, or at the quay shown on the OSI map near a yellow (2004) bungalow. Eastwards from this is a pub and coffee shop by a nice touring caravan park, Hungry Hill Camping Site. Mountain bikes can be hired here. A side lane leads to an old graveyard with the tomb of a Puxley, whose family du Maurier used for her novel. The stone circle shown on the map is worth a visit. Further on is Peg's Stores. To view the many lakes and the Kenmare River it is 7km from the crossroads to the summit of Healy Pass, named after the first Governor-General of the Free State.

The main pier has alongside water and a slip much used by dinghy sailors. The sailing school can spare a small amount of diesel by can and has showers during school hours. Coffee and local knowledge are usually available. The school has two small cruisers. Nearby is a small supermarket (selling Camping Gaz) and a post-office. By the road to Drumlave is an excellent craft shop, Adrigole Arts, which only displays the finest of Irish crafts and original paintings. Drumlave has two pubs and a standing-stone in the field above the chapel. The road up to the Beara Way from Drumlave then back to the harbour, passes more standing stones with views over the harbour to Bear Island and Trafrask Bay.

BEAR ISLAND

LONEHORT HARBOUR

Tides HW as CTB

Lonehart Harbour on Bear Island's south shore is beautiful, lonely and not difficult to enter. From Adrigole it is possible to plot tracks between drying Doucallia and Roancarrigmore lighthouse. The apparent red rock to the north is a wrecked fishing vessel! Sheltered Lonehort is a mile southwest of Lonehort Point but the entrance is difficult to spot. To the south, on Leaghern's Point, are the butts (a long mound) of a rifle range. Head for the small beach just to the north of this, preferably near LW when most rocks are exposed. The narrow island to port on entering, judging by its vegetation, rarely covers. To starboard is a long reef marked by floating weed. The aerial photograph shows all this well and why, with a least depth of 1.8m, it is easiest to enter near low water. When past the rocks extending into the channel from the narrow island's eastern end, head for the electricity pole (with transformer) to the northwest, then swing around (over sand) the end of the reef to starboard keeping 50 yards off the north shore.

Anchor, over a patch of sand, in the bight to the east near a fishing vessel mooring –

sheltered from any wind. It is possible to land nearby but this means a marshy scramble to the road above. The best landing is at the other end, then climb past a field with a rusty shed to the same road into Rerrin. The Irish army use this road frequently so you may get a lift. Bear Island's sights and facilities are covered later under Lawrence Cove Marina.

THE SOUTHERN SIDE OF BEAR ISLAND TO DUNBOY BAY

The southern hillsides of Bear Island are probably the most unspoilt in West Cork. Apart from the Martello Tower there are few dwellings. Sheep graze cols in the wild hillside. (Watch for offshore rocks too!) In the distance Black Ball Head, with its tower, rises then falls sharply into the sea. Mountains on Beara rise above Bear Island. To the northwest is Knockagour. It overlooks Castletownbere with the CGR and RTÉ aerials which give such good coverage in Bantry Bay and the Kenmare River. (However, CTB has a dedicated FM frequency for RTE Radio 1.) Above Shee Head the white lighthouse on Ardnakinna Point just shows.

Lonehort Harbour, Bear Island

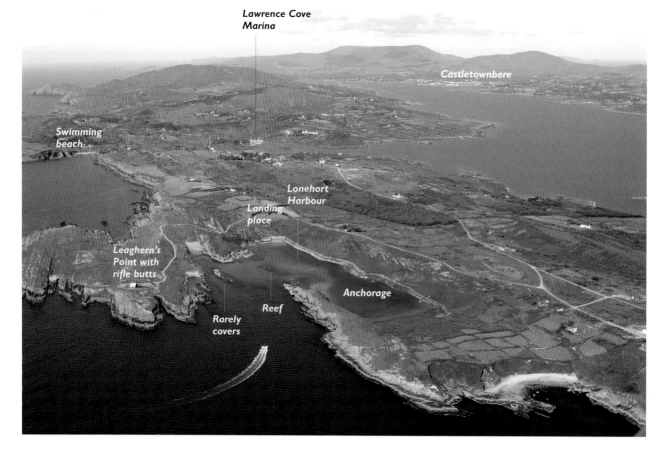

DUNBOY BAY

Tides HW as CTB

Entering Piper Sound the west shore is bare but beyond Piper's Point it is densely wooded. A zigzag path runs up from the lighthouse then down to a little quay just beyond Naglas Point, linking with the Beara Way. The sound then widens with Colt Rock, with its red horse mark, lies ahead. Before this, turn west past dangerous Dunboy Rock for the shallow creek leading to Dunboy House – once the home of the Puxleys. This house was fired in 1922, as described in *Hungry Hill*, but the roofless shell is well preserved. The anchorage just north of ruined Dunboy Castle is very beautiful. Drying Dunboy Rock lies just NE of this anchorage. A missing perch had been replaced (2004) by a red mooring-like buoy! For a visual clearing transit for this rock keep the front door of Dunboy House open to the left of a solitary ash tree on the grass foreshore (the photo shows this well). There is another anchorage, again in mud, to the north at the entrance to Traillan Harbour.

Land at the small beach below O'Sullivan Bere's castle; the grassy mounds of its lower walls make a good picnic spot. There are also the remains of a star-shaped English fort. Behind Dunboy House is a riding stable; enquire at a house at the entrance to Dunboy. The pier in front of the house is unusable. Pulleen Harbour is an easy 3km walk or cycle past farms, marsh and lakes. A stream from these tumbles down a salmon and sea trout

ladder cut in the low cliff by the Puxleys. Another road leads to the entrance of Piper Sound, with steps down to an angling hotspot.

Colt Rock ahead, marked by a red horse, north of the entrance to Dunboy Bay (see plan page 82)

Dunboy House from the anchorage off ruined Dunboy Castle. Note the front door of the house open to the left of the solitary ash tree on the grass foreshore. This transit clears drying Dunboy Rock lying just NE of this anchorage

Castletown. Piper Sound

Dunboy
House

Ruin of
Dunboy Castle

Dunboy Rock

Alternative
anchorage

Traillan
Harbour

**Castletown.
Dunboy Bay**

BEARHAVEN

MILL COVE

Mill Cove is a peaceful anchorage on the north shore of Bearhaven. Proceeding east from CTB note the ferry terminal tucked in behind Sheep Islands on Bear Island. When past Walter Scott SCM (page 82) pick up the back bearing of 245° shown on the charts and plan. Rounding Hornet Rock SCM, leave the wreck (marked by a NCM) to starboard, and head for the narrow entrance to Mill Cove between two reefs. (The *Bardini Reefer* was an eastern bloc fish-factory which caught fire, then sank, in 1984 when new owners started

**The wrecked
Bardini Reefer in
Bear Haven,
from W**

the engine.) Entering the cove from the east beware of drying rocks (not on the chart) east of Illaunboudane, beyond an old Admiralty pier with flagstaff. Keeping the face of the pier open clears these. At LW all is revealed but at HW keep nearer to the western entrance. There is just 2m in very clear water over mud inside the heads. The foreshore is littered with boulders so do not sound further in. Bearhaven Golf Club's nine-hole course straddles the stream entering the head of the bay. The club (☎ 027 71957) welcomes, without formality, sailors desirous of a stout – and possibly a round of golf – and has parking for visiting motor caravans. Land in the creek behind Sea Point. The ferry terminal for Rerrin (Lawrence Cove, Bear Island) in Beal Lough is just beyond the clubhouse, past the haven's disused concrete arsenal.

This anchorage gives views of the coastal plateau and mountains of Beara and the southern slopes of Bear Island. These are beautiful when the furze is in full bloom. On Knocanallig's summit is the white Marian Cross (to the Virgin Mary) erected in 1950. In late May the calls of mating cuckoos on the island were almost deafening, and unfurling the main in Mill Cove disturbed several large moths. With no agriculture and just a few cattle and sheep, Bere – as spelt by the locals – is one of the most accessible islands for observing birds in Cork and Kerry.

LAWRENCE COVE MARINA

Tides HW as CTB

(This beautiful marina has dropped the apostrophe after 'Lawrence'.) There is no longer a buoyed channel. Initially keep closer to the western side of the entrance if the 2.7m rock on the chart and plan concerns you. The marina is easy to enter with sufficient water on the outside pontoons and close to the pontoons at the head of the creek. Turn in past the detached pier at the western end of the reef, with the yellow buoy and rusty tank in the photograph. (Turk Island is not so conspicuous as in this telephoto picture – see also the plan and photo in ISDs). A post with a cross marks a rock just off the seaward end of the pontoons. The diesel berth is at this end of the first pontoon. Tie up there if you need fuel. You will be met, fuelled and allocated a berth by one of the family who built and own the marina. This is a very popular stop for charter yachts, which generally night-stop for showers and an evening in the pub, with a meal in nearby Kitty's Café. This serves excellent food and wines at a very reasonable price.

A good anchorage is between the visitors' moorings and the shore, in the cove inside Ardagh Point. At HW it is also possible to go alongside the old quay with a ladder outside the reef on the east side of Lawrence's Cove. This dries to rock but is only a short walk to Rerrin for shopping, the post office and Des O'Sullivan's pub. The tramway on this quay was for transporting stores and munitions for

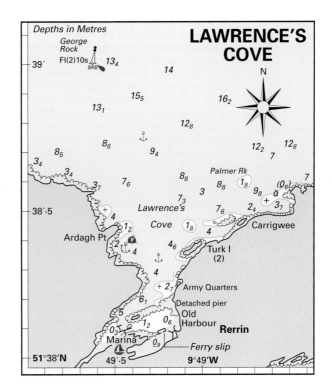

this once-fortified island; the terminal on the mainland was the pier at Mill Cove. The sailing school has gone, and the house where the British Admiral kept his glass on the fleet is now a hostel.

The reef can only be crossed by very shallow-draught craft, keeping close west of a pole marking the best water. Land on the beach in Rerrin's old harbour. The ferry to the mainland uses a slip there and routes past the marina.

**Lawrence Cove
Marina from SW**

Castletownbere

Mill Cove

Bear Haven

Wreck

Detached quay

Post on reef

Rerrin Old harbour

Quay

Visitors' moorings

**Lawrence Cove
Marina from SE**

IRISH STEW

With thanks to Carolyn King, Marina Manager,
Cahersiveen, Co. Kerry, on whose recipe this is based.

Ingredients for 6

2lb neck end or gigot chops of lamb, cut into thick pieces*

3 onions (or equivalent in succulent Irish leeks)

4-6 good-sized potatoes, peeled and quartered

1 pint brown stock (or water if stock cubes not available)

Chopped parsley, salt and pepper

(Carolyn adds a carrot for each person, adding colour and taste.)

To cook

Place a layer of lamb in a heavy-bottomed saucepan, or casserole dish if you are cooking in the oven. (Do not remove bones as these flavour the gravy and can be removed easily before serving.) Cover with a layer of the onions/leeks (and chopped carrots if used), salt and pepper and a layer of potatoes. Repeat this until all ingredients are used, finishing with a layer of potatoes. Add stock/water and bring to the boil. Simmer gently for about 50 mins (possibly longer if using the oven), until potatoes feel soft. Sprinkle with parsley and serve.

We eat this accompanied by freshly-made Odlum's Quick Bread to soak up the gravy.

*Should you be in Castletownbere, get your meat from the very helpful Collins Butchers, whose shop you will find on the right as you walk westward from SuperValu towards the town square. Like most Irish butchers he really knows his trade.

The marina has excellent ablutions and laundry room, both with a feminine touch. Good wines are sold in the marina's craft shop, which has all the information on the island. The telephone box is needed because mobiles do not work here. There is a slip, 14-tonne boat-lift and a hard.

Motor caravans can park near 19th-century Lonehort Fort. This cannot be entered, but a 6-inch gun can still be seen. The main reason for this and other batteries was to protect 19th-century British dreadnoughts anchored in the haven while they got up steam. (This could take two days.) Nowadays the Irish army use the island for training and the old sailing school as accommodation, with an Officers' Mess nearby.

A short distance south of Rerrin is a gravel and sand beach with a slip for diving from. Nearby is a wedge tomb. The well-preserved Martello Tower on Cloonagh Head is reached by a path which leads up from the road above the beach. The path is entered through the garden of a private dwelling. Near the tower are the remains of the barracks which housed the tower's crew. Martello towers were first built as defences in Britain during the Napoleonic wars. They were conceived by the French, the name coming from the gun tower on Cape Mortella in Corsica which gave the British navy much trouble in 1794. The round, 13ft-thick walls were very difficult to destroy with the naval armament of the day. A long-range, 24-pounder cannon was mounted on the roof. There is a signal tower on the western end of Bere, reached by the Beara Way. This would have been manned by a lieutenant, midshipman, two signallers and five yeoman from a nearby battery.

Whilst clambering to explore this unspoilt island you will find rare fauna thriving in the enclosures of abandoned cottages, and a few rusting cars! Mainland road-test failures come here for their last unlicensed fling before being returned to the mainland for scrap. For crew wishing to stay whilst the skipper explores Bantry Bay, Rerrin has a variety of holiday accommodation, mainly recently built.

TWO SMALL FAIR-WEATHER HAVENS WEST OF BEAR ISLAND

Note These two harbours are only for very settled weather.

PULLEEN HARBOUR

Tides HW as CTB

This deep-water inlet in the cliffs is just west of Bear Island. From Fair Head the cliffs are heavily eroded. Just before Pulleen is a cliff – like a layer cake – of grey, brown and white rock; just after this are three modern, cliff-top dwellings. Keeping to the centre of the narrow cleft leading to the harbour, there is ample water all the way into a cliff-bound pool with about 5m just beyond the 8.2m sounding. The main hazard is the many pots all the way from the entrance. *Balair* anchored with her fisherman, swinging comfortably in this really wild and beautiful place. Early next morning a large billy-goat was inspecting this intruder into his domain.

BLACK BALL HARBOUR

Tides HW Cóbh –0100

This is a much wider inlet facing southwest just beyond Black Ball Head, where rare volcanic rock is dark compared with White Ball Head across the entrance. Both from land and at anchor the harbour is very beautiful. The south shores slope up to a well-preserved watch tower while the other shore is low with a new quay and a few dwellings. It must have been a remote landing place for contraband as well as fish. *Balair* motored in close to the north shore with no problem; there is plenty of water as far as the quay. Past this, much weed rises to the surface and there are small craft moorings. Fishing vessels moor in the deeper water to seaward leaving plenty

Black Ball Harbour from NE
Joy Swanson

of anchoring room. They use the quay frequently but it is possible to go alongside at HW.

A gentle climb through sheep-grazed pastures leads to the tower with views to Dursey Island. This would be a pleasant day anchorage while awaiting the tides for Dursey Sound or rounding Dursey Head.

THE COAST TO DURSEY ISLAND

Crossing the bay to Crow Head, the coast and hinterland slope up and east back to the aerials on Knockgour, which will continue to be conspicuous from the Kenmare River. If tide and wind suit, it is safe to pass inside Cat Rock, off Crow Head, before rounding Bull's Forehead for Dursey Sound or proceeding to round Dursey Head, both covered in the following section.

4 DURSEY HEAD TO VALENTIA

Darrynane Harbour in the Kenmare
River looking over Hog's Head to
Ballinskelligs Bay

4 DURSEY HEAD TO VALENTIA

Ports, harbours and anchorages

Garnish Bay – Ballycrovane – Sneem

Cleanderry – Ardgroom – Kilmakilloge

Coongar Harbour – Blackwater Harbour – Dunkerron Harbour – Kenmare Harbour – Dinish Island – Ormond's Island – West Cove – Darrynane Harbour – Ballinskelligs – Portmagee – Valentia Harbour – Cahersiveen Marina

Arrival ports

Castletownbere or Valentia (Cahersiveen Marina)

Charts and maps

Passage and planning charts
Imray C56 or AC 2424, 2423
Essential large-scale chart
AC 2495
Others AC 2125
OSI Discovery Series maps 84, 85

Coastguard radio relay station and MRSC with working channels

Bantry Ch 23
Valentia MRSC
VHF Ch 23 MF 1752kHz

RNLI Lifeboats

Castletownbere, Valentia

Important landfall lights

The Bull
Great Skellig
Valentia
Fort (Cromwell) Point

Tourist information

Cork Kerry Tourism, Aras Failte, Grand Parade, Cork
☎ 021 4273251 *Fax* 021 4273504
Email info@corkkerrytourism.ie
www.ireland.travel.ie

A BRIEF DESCRIPTION OF THE AREA

The greater part of this area is the Kenmare River. For this the coastal cruiser must be well victualled and fully fuelled. There are many wild, rock-strewn and beautiful anchorages, but only Kenmare, now an almost disused port, has convenient shopping. Another problem when cruising north of Dursey is that the Atlantic swell is now more pronounced. This sometimes makes reef-bound harbours unapproachable, but Kenmare is a narrow river, with havens on either shore. Kenmare partly dries but there is a pool, scoured by the Roughty River, with 2-3m. Holding is good but this is not recommended at springs, after heavy inland rain, because of the strong ebbs. A safe alongside berth is possibly for the night, or for a short shopping trip. For those with time, who are prepared to anchor and make some effort to get groceries, a thorough exploration of this unspoilt ria should not be missed. Fresh water, by can or alongside, is no problem.

Arriving from the south, Castletownbere is the port for victualling, then refuelling at nearby Lawrence Cove Marina. This is described in Section 3. From the north, Valentia, with upstream Cahersiveen Marina, is an excellent arrival port. The submarine telegraph cables of Ballinskelligs Bay are now part of communication history. It is possible to anchor just southwest of Waterville, which has good shopping, but there is no landing place other than the shingle beach. This can get breakers from Atlantic swell. Large Lough Currane, world famous for its salmon, drains into this anchorage. Another famous salmon river, the Inny, enters north of the rocks off Waterville so salmon nets, legal or otherwise, are a hazard from June onwards. Salmon rivers also enter the Ri]ver, at Sneem and Kenmare. Waterville is a pleasant town

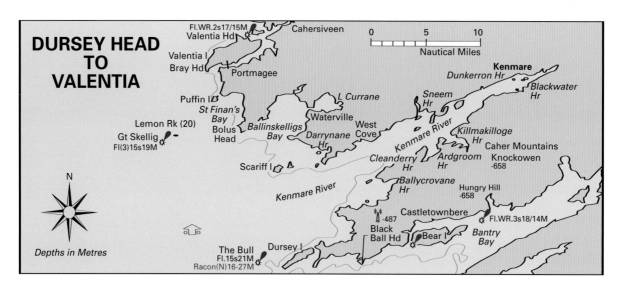

and a favoured lunch stop for tourists going around the Ring of Kerry.

A description of Valentia is left to the end of this section, as that is also the best arrival port for Dingle Bay and Peninsula.

INTO THE KENMARE RIVER

Tides HW Dursey is approx. HW Cóbh –0050
Height 00.5m

Outbound on this coastal recce, the strategy (with knowledge of where stores were available) was to criss-cross the Kenmare as victuals, winds and weather dictated.

DURSEY SOUND

Tidal streams
N-going begins HW Cóbh +0135
S-going begins HW Cóbh begins –0450
Max rates 4kn

Balair chose to take Dursey Sound near neaps, in a light easterly, entering just before the northwest stream started. The cable car across the sound gives a vertical clearance of 21 metres over the narrows. There can be eddies and overfalls in the narrows between the island and rocks on the mainland side. The deepest and best water is close to the island and there can be marked wind shifts, particularly at the sound's northern end. To await smooth water there is an anchorage, in 10m, off the quay shown on the chart. *Balair* headed from Crow Head (see Section 3) towards the signal tower on Dursey, until a course could be laid to pass between Old Breaker and Illanebeg, at the southern entrance of the sound.

ROUND DURSEY HEAD

Tidal streams
N-going begins HW Cóbh +0235
S-going begins HW Cóbh –0350
Up to 3kn at springs

The route around Dursey Head is more interesting. Only southern Dursey has a few dwellings and farm land. The island is bare and lizard-like from the north (though the reptile could be crawling either way). The northwestern tip has high, eroded cliffs; east of the signal tower the land slopes down to just above the water. There is the base of a square tower on the Head. A cast iron LH, 102 feet high, was first lit on the Calf Rock, with its adjoining Heifer, in 1866 but was partly destroyed in 1881. Part of the brick inner shell remains. The derivation of these English names becomes obvious when the larger Bull and Cow are viewed from the northeast; the Bull (elephant) has legs and a

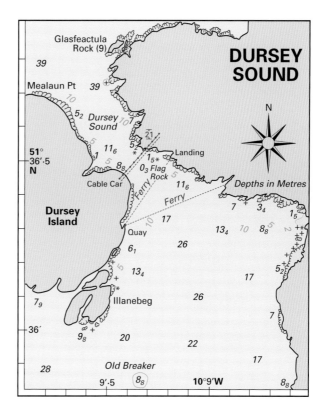

calf tagging along. His mate is complete with tail and trunk. (These names were probably given by a 19th-century surveyor who was familiar with these creatures.) Streams can be strong between Dursey Head and these Islands.

ANCHORAGES ON THE SOUTHERN SHORE OF THE KENMARE

Balair motor-sailed through the sound – in May it was too early for salmon nets – then motored into wind for Garnish Bay (51°37′N 10°7′W), anchoring just outside the drying slip shown on the chart. The beach is best for landing, but *Balair* was only anchoring for lunch. Approach is on SW between Long Island and a concrete beacon, lining up an isolated farmhouse (green in 2004) with a small beach. Holding is good in sand between patches of weed. Crabber and farmer Patrick O'Sullivan (of the green house) came alongside for a chat and left a crab for supper. The best shelter from west to southeast is the anchorage marked on the chart. Some pots have plastic cans with long floating lines. Stone-walled fields, with grazing sheep and cattle, slope down to little sandy coves. There are no facilities. Dursey's cable car is only 2½km by road or the Beara Way.

Just 3 miles to the east is the white beach at Ballydonegan. This consists of washings from the many disused copper mines on this coast of Beara. There is a good quay where the ore was loaded. With an easterly the

Drying harbour

Beacon

Garnish Bay from SW looking towards Cod's Head at low water. The rocky harbour dries. The beacon is outside the moorings. The white patches are just foam – not rocks

Looking NE towards the white beaches of Ballydonegan, inside Allihies Point
Cork Kerry Tourism

opportunity was taken to anchor that afternoon off this steeply shelving beach, between two reefs. The plan to go ashore next day to view the old mines was thwarted by a forecast of southwest 6 to 7, so it was back to the charted anchorage in Garnish Bay. The CQR held well, in 10m, for two safe but uncomfortable days, with further visits from our farming friend. Although Ballydonegan Bay is exposed, it was fine in the offshore easterly.

Stores were getting low and the pretty village of Eyeries, in Coulagh Bay, has shops and pubs. The small harbour dries and has a pier much used by fishing vessels. It has reefs and rocks outside the entrance. But

Ballycrovane, in the northeast corner of the bay, is less than 3km by road from Eyeries. That would make a nice walk to the shops and a meal ashore for a change. The forecast was still unsettled for the early morning passage around Cod's Head.

Following the chart and plans the entrance to Ballycrovane is simple. Clear of the tracks, just southeast of Innishfarnard, there is a large salmon farm. The final track of 261° is close to a row of four upright stones – just past Reen Point. Give the red beacon on Illaunnameanla a good berth then turn port to anchor south of the old harbour, between the moored yacht and the barge in the photograph. Note the drying reef which is on

From the best sheltered anchorage in Garnish Bay, marked on AC 2495. Stone walled fields with grazing sheep and cattle slope down at LW to little sandy coves

Give the red beacon on Illaunnameanla a good berth before anchoring off the old harbour at Ballycrovane

track between the anchorage and pier. It is very weedy and *Balair* dragged several times before finding good holding – with no evidence of mud.

There are no facilities in this beautiful and wild place. The best landing is at the fishing vessel pier, but there is no rubbish disposal there. The foreshore is weed-covered rock but at HW there is a landing at the old harbour north of the anchorage. (It was not prudent to walk to Eyeries now.) Lough Fadda is an easy walk, as is the ancient site of Kilcatherine Church and the Hag of Beara, a petrified Celtic woman. The upright stones are on the way. Near the new quay is the tallest Ogham Stone (5.3m) in the world; the landowner charges for access. For much more information on the area see the small leaflet *Eyeries and Ardgroom on the Ring of Beara*, available in Castletownbere.

The old harbour and landing place at Ballycrovane

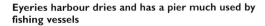

Eyeries harbour dries and has a pier much used by fishing vessels

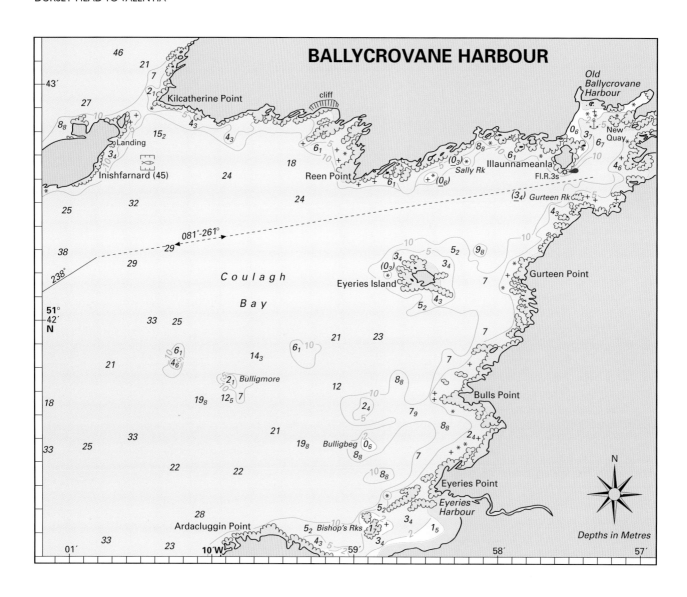

BALLYCROVANE HARBOUR

Old Ballycrovane Harbour

Kilcatherine Point

cliff

New Quay

Landing

Inishfarnard (45)

Reen Point

Sally Rk

Illaunnameanla

Fl.R.3s

Gurteen Rk

C o u l a g h

081°-261°

B a y

238°

51°
42′
N

Eyeries Island

Gurteen Point

Bulls Point

Bulligmore

Bulligbeg

Eyeries Point

Eyeries Harbour

Ardacluggin Point

Bishop's Rks

10 W

N

Depths in Metres

Looking **SW** from Ballycrovane towards Eyeries and Cod's Head

Red beacon

Barge

Drying reef

Anchorage

Old harbour

New quay

ACROSS THE KENMARE TO SNEEM

After a surfeit of rock-strewn anchorages, with fresh food and water low, Sneem Harbour beckoned from across the water. This large estuarial harbour, protected by islands, has many safe anchorages and there are visitors' moorings. Fresh food is available, with a little effort. Alongside water is at refurbished Oyster House quay. As usual, there is no rubbish disposal.

Leaving Ballycrovane, swell made conditions unsuitable for the short cut between Kilcatherine Point and Inishfarnard Island. Breakers also meant a considerable diversion to the southwest around Sticken Rock. With good visibility it was quicker to enter Sneem by the alternative entrance north of Sherky Island. The grey pointed tower of the conspicuous hotel, showing above trees, makes a good pilotage mark. Soundings are useful back-up, especially for the shallow spit after Potato Island. Past this it is safe to turn port for the inner anchorages. The main entrance is between Sherky with its adjoining islands and Rossdohan Island. Entering from the east, keep outside the 30m depth contour as the reef off Rossdohan Island can have breakers out to 20m – even in a moderate swell.

Anchoring between two concrete beacons and Rossdohan is convenient for famous Parknasilla Hotel and a delightful little fishing quay shown as a pier on OSI 84. On the chart it is where the road crosses to Rossdohan Island. This is only suitable for a tender. A night was spent there in the campervan. Anchoring between Garinish Island and Oyster House quay is handier for victualling, with better views. Visitors' moorings are in the bight to the northeast. Local moorings make it difficult to anchor in the bay on the northeast side of Garinish. This also gets wash from traffic to and from the island's houses.

A good run ashore by tender is to the magnificent Parknasilla Hotel (☎ 1850 383848 or 064 45122 www.gshparknasilla.com). There may be rock-basking seals on route. Perches mark the drying reefs on the approach seen in the photograph. It is best to land on the beach on the outside of the quay. Yachtsmen should make themselves known; they will be welcome but should not wear yachting gear. The bar has free small eats, and ice for the boat's box is given willingly. Meals are also available. To take advantage of all the facilities – golf, croquet, heated swimming pool and walks in the hotel's extensive sub-tropical gardens – it is necessary to take at least a day room. Some of the crew may desert ship here!

SNEEM

The most exciting way to shop in Sneem is by tender. Do not attempt this without a motor as it is at least 2 nautical miles, not including wrong turnings. So take a compass, OSI 84 and head for a sugar-loaf mountain. Reefs and rocks are marked by long weed and the currents are strong in places. The best view of Sneem is from the river; lovely mountains make a backdrop to attractive buildings and

Sneem Harbour and the river to Sneem village. Parknasilla hotel is on the right

A delightful little fishing quay at Rossdohan, Sneem Harbour

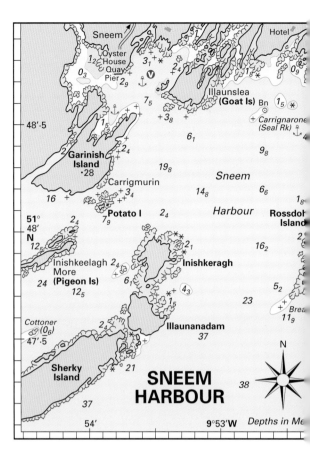

Parknasilla Hotel, Sneem

churches. This village clusters around a pleasant green, but maybe too much coloured paint has been slapped on some house fronts.

A low quay below Sneem has rubbish disposal. Shopping is a short walk alongside a public garden. Enterprising John Christian has a 'seven-day' grocery. In the sailing season he posts details of his taxi service on Oyster Quay (☎ 064 45116 or mobile ☎ 087 244 9026). Sneem is 4km by road from this quay. John accepts all major credit cards and has a cash machine. There are other stores: butcher, pharmacist, hardware with Camping Gaz, and a post office. Excellent woollen goods are also available. Banks open on Tuesdays or Thursdays. A game fishing river tumbles out of the mountains through Sneem (permits available from the tourist office). The pub for thirsty shoppers is the The Blue Bull.

BACK TO THE SOUTH SIDE OF THE KENMARE

CLEANDERRY HARBOUR

Four miles southwest of Sneem, Cleanderry (Cleandra) Harbour is the largest of the two rockbound inlets 2½ miles southwest of Ardgroom. Initially locate the 9-yard wide entrance, on a back bearing of 026° to Parknasilla Hotel over the eastern shore of Illaunanadan. The entrance, through a reef, is difficult to see, but entry is safe and easy near LW when there is at least 1.8m. Approaching the coast, look for a large grey house with tall pine trees on each side. This house on 205°, with a lichen-yellow island to starboard, is a good final track for the entrance. This is confirmed by mussel barrels beyond the reefs. The second of the two reefs inside is very close to, and merges with, the shore. Keep the first reef (the southern extension of a narrow creek) about 50 yards to port whilst turning on to an easterly heading using the barrels as a SHM. The second reef is well clear to starboard. Anchor at the eastern end off a small new quay. The photograph shows all this well. Mussels are offloaded at the other end of the harbour. The quay gives direct access to the Beara Way and cycle route. Overlooked by a few houses, with a southwest breeze outside, this made a calm and peaceful lunch stop, with half a cable of swinging room. The anchor and chain gathered a trace of mud.

Sneem Harbour. Anchorage NE of Garinish Island

Approaching Cleanderry, with large grey house with tall pine trees on either side on 205°, with a lichen-yellow island to starboard. Note mussel barrels beyond the entrance

Cleanderry Harbour from the SW. There is 1.8m in the narrow entrance (confirmed by echo sounder). The barrels make a good SHM for approaching the anchorage – outside the moored boats

ONWARD TO ARDGROOM FOR TEA

ARDGROOM HARBOUR

Do not be deterred by the hectares of mussel barrels that at first seem to cover huge Ardgroom Harbour completely. Good binoculars and a bearing compass are essential to find some of the five beacons leading around to the anchorage off Pallas Harbour. It is advisable to have engine and anchor ready before entering. Refer to ISDs for the many off-track hazards.

The conspicuous black beacon by Halftide Rock is aligned on 135° for the initial approach. Keep the next white beacon on 099° until the rear white beacon has been positively identified. This is partly obscured by vegetation and only its top shows at first. (Several white chimneys are more conspicuous!) The next two beacons, to be aligned astern on 026°, are very difficult to pick out. The front still has some black paint but the rear is camouflaged by the rocks behind. A whitish line of rock, resembling a stone wall, leads down behind it at 45°. However, a back bearing of 026° on the white beacon is safe. Barrels ahead necessitate turning starboard for the quay a little sooner than recommended in ISDs. Following this farm's seaward edge clears the shallows to the north before turning on to about 300° for the large new quay. There is a good anchorage just south of this between the shore and two sets of barrels (see photograph).

AROUND THE UNNAMED POINT TO KILMAKILLOGE HARBOUR

Before departing from Ardgroom note the smooth grassy fields above Pallas harbour. As at Sneem, you are now entering the post ice-age estuary of the Kenmare River, with eroded 'grassy cliffs' shown on the charts. Upstream the banks become progressively more pastoral or wooded. You are also passing from the waters of Cork into those of Kerry. This upper Kenmare River could be renamed the Ria of Small Island Anchorages: nature has gouged many bays on both coasts,

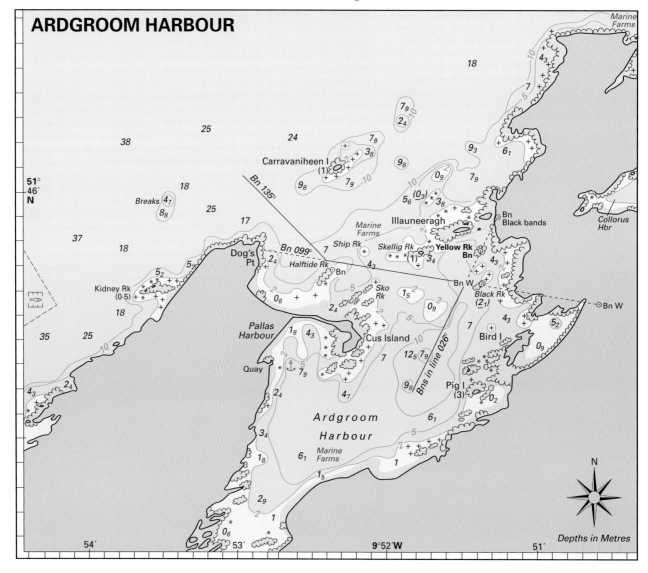

Sherky
Island

Beacon
Halftide
Rock

New quay
and slip

Anchorage

leaving them protected by long, thin islands. A yacht could spend many days exploring these attractive desert islands; but supper-time camp fires or BBQs are needed to keep the midges of high summer at bay.

KILMAKILLOGE HARBOUR

From Ardgroom's Halftide Rock beacon it is possible to pass between Carravaniheen reef and the marine farms. Kilmakilloge ('Kilmacilow' with emphasis on 'mac') has everything the traditional cruising person wants. There are many sheltered anchorages, all easily reached despite many mussel farms. For some there may be too many conifers and rhododendrons in the upper parts of the harbour.

Head first for Bunaw Harbour, hidden behind a grassy cliff. This has long been a favourite watering hole for Irish sailors. Approach on a track of 105° from the western entrance point (as shown on the plan) leaving a gravel mound (Spanish Island) to starboard. Mussel barrels just after this necessitate an earlier interception of the 041° leading line into Bunaw. This is marked by

Ardgroom from SE. A good anchorage is between the mussel farms SW of the new quay at Reenavade

Bunaw's anchorage, bounded by meadows and low cliffs, could be in England's west country but for the mountains

Breakwater submerged
at HW

Slip

Coongar
Harbour

Rocks

**Bunaw Harbour,
Kilmakilloge,
from the S at
LW**

black poles, with yellow stripes and conspicuous white electronic boxes. These supply leading lights – but only for locals. The front mark is on the pier. Limited anchorage is between the pier head and the spit to the west where mussel boats dry out. Keep just outside the moorings, and half a cable from the pier because of rocks. The meadows and low cliffs of this anchorage, with its adjacent stone breakwater, could be in England's west country – were it not for the mountains to the east.

Do not land at the old slip outside the pier (rocks) and beware of a submerged breakwater protecting the slip inside the pier. At HW keep close by the steps on the pier if landing on this slip. Note the high concrete grid at the base of the pier if going alongside. There are no ladders. Teddy O'Sullivan's bar will supply water in cans and take a small amount of rubbish. Mrs Helen Moriarty has owned this long-established family pub since the 1970s. The drinkers' part of the bar is very old and has been extended to cater for

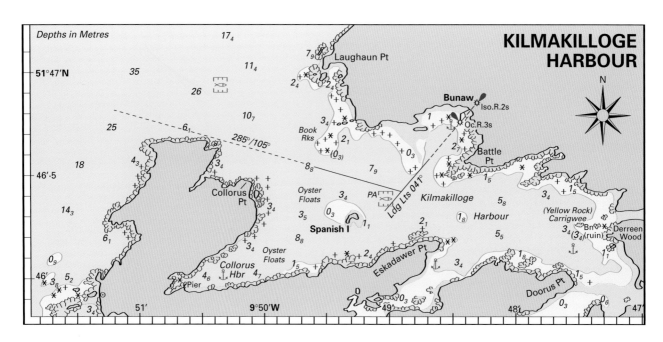

the many walkers. Helen provides B&B, meals and limited provisions (☎ 064 83104). The nearest shops are at Laura (3km), passing Derreen Gardens. An interesting walk is over the hills behind the pub, then down the valley of a trout stream to join Lansdowne Road. His Lordship had much property locally, besides that better known sporting venue in Dublin. Initially overhung with deciduous trees, Lansdowne Road follows the coast back to Bunaw past Lehid Harbour. That reef-bound anchorage was not for *Balair*.

Derreen Gardens have a nearby anchorage just south of Carrigwee. Both the bay south of Escadawer Point and deeper Collorus Harbour are attractive anchorages with convenient landings – Collorus has a quay. These are easily approached around or between mussel farms.

One afternoon *Balair* visited all these anchorages, as well as Coongar Harbour on the other side of the Kenmare, Blackwater Harbour at the mouth of the Blackwater River, and finally Dunkerron Harbour just below Kenmare (see photograph on page 116 for location of Coongar Harbour).

TO KENMARE

COONGAR HARBOUR

To the northeast of the entrance there is a fairly large green buoy guarding Maiden Rock – in mid-river. At the head of the harbour are three small sets of mussel barrels. Beyond these, behind a reef, is a small quay backed by three houses. The only facilities are

a Roman Catholic church and a post box. By road it is 4km to Parknasilla and 8km to Sneem. Outside the 5m depth contour, as the stone bridge to Rossmore Island comes into view, would make a very attractive anchorage – preferably negotiated at LW.

BLACKWATER HARBOUR

A radio mast rises just beyond the narrow wooded entrance, 3 miles northwest of Coongar Harbour. A low steamer quay has a few small craft alongside. There are local moorings and no signs of fishing vessels. (No inspection from ashore was made on the recce by road.) A sheltered anchorage just outside the pier is recommended.

DUNKERRON HARBOUR

Further upstream the channel narrows between rocky spits off both shores. Drying Carrignaroneebeg has a post topped with a red basket. To starboard a conspicuous round stone pillar on Reennaveagh, when on 245° or less, clears rocks off that shore. Turreted Dromore Castle is part-hidden by trees on the north shore. The long white pier at the eastern end of the harbour may show between islands to the southwest of Dunkerron, but do not take this passage. To enter the harbour, clear Bowlings Rock before rounding Illaungowla, leaving drying Cod Rock to port and the reef off Fox Island to starboard. In 2003 and 2004 a large ketch was moored in the anchorage marked on the chart. (This

Blackwater Harbour from inside the pier at HW

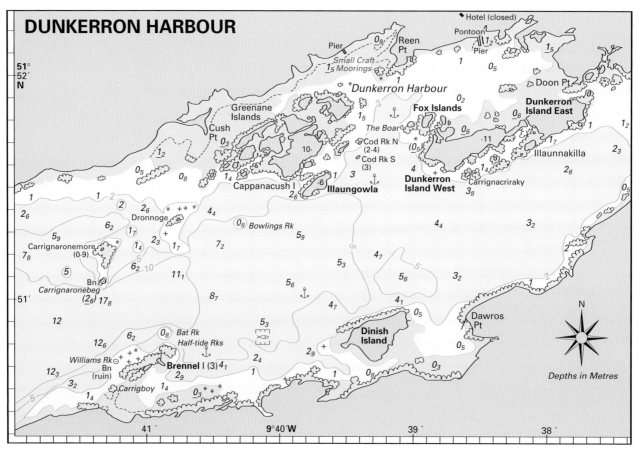

DUNKERRON HARBOUR

Depths in Metres

Dunkerron Harbour. Looking W towards Blackwater Harbour and Sneem

possibly belonged to the hotel, which closed after the owner died.) Last surveyed in 1854 and 1900, the harbour had, in 2004, considerably more water than charted. There is good holding in 2.4m just west of the long white pier. The mud is black and messy.

In 2004 it was possible to go alongside the hotel's long quay, which has a water tap. A good beach to dry out is between this pier and a pontoon. These facilities were part of a

marina but with redevelopment all could change, including use of the 1km driveway to the main road. At the road entrance there is a long-established riding school offering lessons (☎ 064 41043).

The touring caravan park shown on OSI is excellent. (Ring of Kerry Caravan and Camping Park ☎ 064 41648.) For basic groceries visit this before 1000 or in the late afternoon. Beyond is the well-marked Kerry

Ruan pier

Ketch (in 2004)

Water on pier

Pontoon

Way to Kenmare town, over hills with views of the upper Kenmare River. Dunkerron is a 'Bay of Islands'. The two large and well-wooded islands to the south call out to be explored.

The quay at Ruan, on the mainland to the west shown on the chart and photograph – with boats moored off – is in excellent condition for going alongside and drying out. A kilometre to the west, along the nearby road, there is a good pub serving meals.

KENMARE HARBOUR

At half flood there is a push of up to 1 knot for the final leg to Kenmare Harbour. Keep close to the north shore's islands, now grazed by goats, cattle and horses. Past these is a large new house fronted by a boulder quay. From here, head for the end of Kenmare pier. Approaching this poles mark the northern edge of the drying mud spit. The harbour east of the pier dries; marked by a half-tide post. The large Roughty River gouges a deep pool (2.5m) below the concrete suspension bridge. There are moorings here. At springs or after heavy rains anchor just to the north to avoid very strong ebbs. There is no major commercial fishing activity.

Raymond Ross, skipper and owner of *Seafaris*, runs tours from the pier head. He is very helpful and yachts may use his permanent pontoon to fill with water or for shopping when he is out on a tour. (SuperValu ☎ 064 41307 delivers to the pier.) Raymond's 'Eco Tours' take about 2 hours and he gives

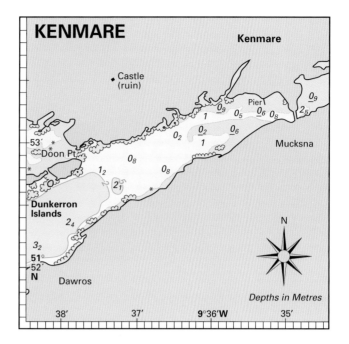

an excellent commentary. Customers get maps, binoculars, snacks and complimentary refreshments. He can be contacted on ☎ 064 83171 or at his cottage, No 3 (with the stone seals) at the base of the pier. By arrangement yachts may dry out by *Seafaris* for the night. Raymond will direct strangers approaching or leaving Kenmare (if it looks necessary!)

KENMARE TOWN

Its Irish name Neidín, meaning Little Nest, well describes neat Kenmare. Sir William Petty designed the town around a triangle of roads. It is an easy walk to good shops, pubs

Kenmare Harbour from the SW at LW

Kenmare Post Office has internet and office services

Kenmare's Stone Circle, orientated for the equinox, with a Boulder Dolmen at its centre, is the largest in SW Ireland

and restaurants; arrive at the Wednesday market by 0800. The Lansdowne Arms is the place for a quiet drink, with nice meals in a variety of settings. For an evening of stout, fun, music and song try Crowleys – a long-established family bar which has yet to install a TV! It is sad that this lovely town gets so few visiting yachts.

Above the bridge is the usual tidal lagoon with a nature reserve. Five OSI maps are needed for the many roads and tracks radiating from this important crossing of the ways of Southwest Kerry. The town has a well-preserved stone circle and an interesting 'modern' history which is told in the Tourist Office. Next door is the Lace Centre. Lace has long been a local cottage industry. You can see it being made by hand, buy it and also admire antique lace in the centre. (The shops in town only sell machine-made stuff.) The picturesque harbour has a fringe of grass, with seats for tired tourists on the town side; trees overhang the southern side. A secluded spot for a picnic or sunbathe is on the north side of the road bridge, where three stone figures gaze out towards the setting sun. There is a small landing beach just below. Kenmare's 18-hole golf course, in the Roughty valley, is a few minutes' walk from town.

Kenmare's Henry Street and RC Church of the Holy Cross

MORE ANCHORAGES ON THE SOUTHERN SHORE OF THE KENMARE

Proceeding downstream two hours after HW there was plenty of water after Dunkerron Island East to head southwest for Dinish Island which has sheltered anchorages on either side. Dinish has a few houses amongst trees. On the east side a steel barge is moored by a pier which appears to be used by fishing vessels. Dawros Point has a pier. The rock, inside the drying area marked on the chart, has a white post.

The western anchorage is much more attractive. A stone quay and a large building by the road were under construction in 2004. The chart shows an anchorage at about 51°58′N 09°40′.6W – just east of Half-Tide Rocks – sheltered from the west by Brennel Island and its half-tide rocks. Further west, large metal drums mark dismantled fish farms and there are many 'amateur' pots with plastic-can floats.

Behind the reefs off the eastern end of Ormond's Island, three miles to the southwest, is a quay (only shown on OSI 84) with moorings for local yachts. The anchorage is entered from the west between humped-back Hog Island to the south and the dangerous rocks off red-soiled Ormond's Island. Hog is hugged before turning to starboard to anchor on the 5m sounding. At

LW this is all quite easy. There must be good trout fishing in the three loughs beyond the main road: the map shows Red Trout Lake. Of several long walks, one is to the rock-bound Lehid Harbour, already mentioned under Bunaw Harbour.

BACK TO THE NORTHERN SHORE

The day's voyage had been planned to end at West Cove, 7 miles west of Sneem, but with a freshening southwesterly and a Small Craft Warning a diversion was made into Sneem. *Balair* sheltered there for two days. When the winds subsided there were but three days before Joy was due to join ship in Cahersiveen. This meant sailing past West Cove and Darrynane Harbour on the next passage to Ballinskelligs. However, these two lovely old staging and trading ports are described now.

WEST COVE

Departure from Sneem was north of Sherky Island before setting course for the reefs to the east of West Cove. Bunnow Harbour, 2½ miles west of Sherky Island, is a small boat harbour and there is said to be a sheltered anchorage behind Illaundrane Island, just to the southwest, but neither of these was investigated by land or sea.

West Cove from SE at LW

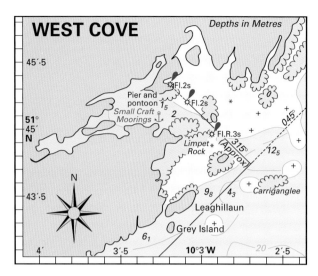

Staigue Fort near West Cove has beautiful stonework, probably dating from the early Christian era

West Cove from the southeast looks very attractive; but how did schooners and steamers get past those reefs? The entrance, for the first time visitor, is from the southwest. There is only room for a few average-size yachts to anchor, in 1.5m to 2m, though boats that are able to take the ground can do so amongst local craft. Once inside, it is very snug. The quay has a landing pontoon used by angling boats. Castle Cove, less than 2km by road, has a store and a pub. Another 5km by road takes you to well-preserved Staigue Fort. West Cove has lovely beaches sheltered from swell at LW by reefs. Looking to the west past low, scrubby and rounded Knocknasullig towards inland mountains it could be a Mediterranean harbour, but just north of the anchorage is lovely Georgian West Cove House. Old roofless buildings to the east are all that remain of a hospital built

in 1912 by the Honourable Albinia Brodrick, one of several aristocratic English ladies who took the side of the Republicans. Du Maurier used this surname for the mine-masters in *Hungry Hill*.

WEST COVE PILOTAGE

Tides LW Cobh –0010

It is best to enter/leave harbours near LW on this part of the coast.

Good visibility is essential, as is a reliable engine, with smooth water between the reefs. Approaching from the west, pick up the inbound track for the initial leading marks (045°) situated south of Castle Cove. This is when GPS, used in navigational mode, is useful with one of the marks as a WP, but don't rely on it to miss the rocks. This track

Balair **anchored in West Cove at half tide**

Balair in West Cove near LW

passes close to rocks south of Knocknasullig, which can be double-checked by the distance display. As so often happens, it is much easier near LW when the reefs on each side show and give shelter from any swell.

By Grey Island the grey (not white) beacons ahead should come in. The front is low down on Burnt Island, the rear higher up on the mainland. Now look for the tall white beacon (Fl.R.3s) to port. This marks the northeast end of Limpet Rock, but do not turn for it until another tall white beacon (Fl.2s) further in becomes open east of Limpet Rock. This means overshooting the final leading line of approximately 315° (nothing quite lines up) before turning back to pass close to Limpet Rock to align the tall white beacon with another beacon to the right of a conspicuous white house. Keep this and the tall white beacon in line, turning port onto a westerly heading, just before the tall beacon, towards moored local craft. Only use these lights for a dusk approach.

ONWARD TO DARRYNANE

WHITE STRAND BAY ANCHORAGE

A good day anchorage, sheltered from the west by Lamb's Head, is off the pier shown on OSI 84 at approximately 51°45´.3N 10°06´.1W (on the chart). ISDs call this White Strand Bay; the map Rath Strand. The bay is littered with dangerous rocks so use

White Strand Bay from Wavecrest Touring Caravan site. The road leads down to the slip

visual navigation and only enter near low water, when these will show or have breakers. With a little effort there is good victualling at the excellent touring caravan site (Wavecrest) shown on the map. Accurate navigation, using a bearing from the quay in the bay (shown on the map) is needed to anchor in 10m between Bulligbeg and Carrigbeg, which only show at very low tides. It is a pleasant walk from the quay to the site's shop, which sells everything but beer and spirits, or to the shops and pub in Caherdaniel. Alternatively, anchor off the slip just to the west of the landscaped touring vans (past the holiday vans), then it is a short walk to Wavecrest's shop. This also sells Pádraig Loingsigh's

History of the Parish of Caherdaniel which contains much of interest between Darrynane and Castle Cove. You can also buy this if you walk the 3¹/₂km to Caherdaniel from Darrynane. Wavecrest (☎ 066 9475188 www.wavecrestcamping.com) is ideal for cruise followers on this part of the coast.

DARRYNANE

(Derrynane is the popular spelling but the almanac, charts and maps all use its old name.) This lovely place is now very popular with cruising yachts – and water-skiers – in high summer. At that time quiet and more sheltered West Cove is to be preferred; there the main activity is angling boats and young families enjoying themselves in sailing dinghies.

Visitors' moorings, a pub near the lovely bathing beaches and a water-sports centre are the main attraction for the summer hordes at Darrynane. Daniel O'Connell, the Liberator (of the Catholics) lived at Darrynane House, which is open to the public. He was buried in Dublin, but the family graves in the burial ground on Abbey Island make an interesting search. There are lovely walks to the east with large strands, marshes and lagoons. Searching for the Ogham stone you will come across many rare plants and plenty of wild birds.

DARRYNANE PILOTAGE

Tides See West Cove

Inshore rescue boat

From the south, route either side of Moylaun Island (from the west or east head for Lamb's Head) and pick up the 034° leading line

Darrynane from the SE at LW with Ballinskelligs Bay in the distance. The yachts are mainly on visitors' moorings and the water skier is heading for the unmarked rock! See photo page 105

which has large, conspicuous white marks. Apart from drying Bulligmore, to starboard 3 cables out, there is open water all the way to the narrow entrance, which is between two rocks which always show. Entering the harbour and almost on the leading line is a red brick beacon. Now turn fairly sharply to leave a similar grey brick beacon to starboard. The main hazards in the entrance are pot buoys and exiting yachts not obeying the collisions regulations! If intending to anchor (if it is the silly season) do so nearer the western end of the harbour. Many yachts let go to queue for the visitors' moorings near the beach and old quay, then snag each others' anchors. There is an unmarked rock which dries 0.6m just northwest of the visitors' moorings. The old quay dries completely. Just beneath the leading marks is a new quay and slip, used by fishing vessels.

BALLINSKELLIGS BAY AND THE SKELLIGS

Tidal streams
Run north during the flood into the Kenmare and south with the ebb, at up to 1½kn

The sounds between Two Headed, Moulaun, Deenish and Scariff Islands are suitable for small craft. Keeping the summit of Horse Island (approximately 51°48′N 10°16′W) on 328° well open of Hog's Head will clear the reefs which sometimes break to the west of Moulaun. The other channels are clear of hazards. An unattended net (just a floating line between two buoys) was set off Hog's Head Island and the Pig's Rocks in June 2004 to intercept salmon homing into the Currane and Inny rivers at Waterville.

BALLINSKELLIGS ANCHORAGE

The cable stations at Waterville and Ballinskelligs closed in 1972. Ballinskelligs has a good anchorage just north of Horse Island, outside local moorings. The bottom has large, easily seen, patches of sand. Beware of the reef just north of the ruined abbey. Sheep graze the little stone fields surrounding a white cottage on Horse Island. A row of disused houses (with chimneys) to the south of the pier was the cable station. 3km to the northeast at Dungeagan are two pubs, one with a restaurant, and a post office. An art gallery with a good coffee shop lies at the junction with the R566. About 1km further along the R566 there is a filling station with hardware and groceries.

Ballinskelligs has several well-sited new homes which do not diminish the beauty of

this great bay, backed by lovely mountains. By the restored pier and beyond the castle there are good bathing strands. If sailing over to Waterville note Bay Rock northeast of Horse Island.

THE SKELLIGS

Great and Little Skellig are 8 miles west of Bolus Head and a similar distance from Portmagee, the southern entrance to Valentia. The wild mountainside southwest of Ballinskelligs was home base for the monks on the Skelligs; it was here that they finally settled on the mainland. As the Skelligs open up beyond shattered Bolus Head they look like fairy-tale castles. The south side of Great Skellig slopes up at 045° with a high, pointed pinnacle leaning towards the north. Then it has a slightly lower but similar peak. Little Skellig is a single pyramid, white with gannets and their guano.

Even in settled conditions it is difficult to land on Great Skellig now, as tourist boats queue to do so all day. The best time would be early morning or in the evening of a long summer day. Des Lavelle of Valentia tells all you need to know about them in his book *The Skellig Story*; his photographs are more

Top
Darrynane entrance is much easier at low water!

Above
The burial ground on Abbey Island, Darrynane

The sun sets over Bolus Head with the Skelligs in the distance
Craig McKechnie

than a substitute for a visit on foot. A visit to the Skellig Experience at Portmagee compliments Lavelle's book. These remote piles of rock are more interesting seen from a few cables off. This avoids close encounters with tour boats milling around close in. Little Skellig, with many 'see through' caves, has the second largest gannetry in the British Isles. To withstand the shock of its dive-bombing attacks the gannet has, amongst other protective devices, air-bag shock absorbers!

The Skelligs' huge spikes are slices of near-vertical strata. The same formation can be seen along the coast from Bolus Head to Portmagee, with many mini-skelligs bedded in the cliffs, particularly so north of Puffin Island. The soundings from Bolus Head and Puffin Island to the Skelligs indicate that this was once a much larger peninsula.

Ballinskelligs anchorage with Puffin Island in the distance, taken from the SE at LW

Horse Island from the anchorage at Ballinskelligs

TOWARDS VALENTIA

PORTMAGEE

From the south the shortest route into Valentia Harbour was through the Portmagee Channel, south of the island. The swing bridge was not opening in 2004; however, this pretty fishing village should not be missed. There are visitors' moorings and good anchorages.

PUFFIN ISLAND

Three miles south of the entrance to Portmagee is Puffin Island, uninhabited apart from birds. Parts are covered with turf, ideal for puffin and shearwater nesting burrows. The only possible landing is on rocks in Boat Cove south of Oats Island, in fair weather with west to northwest wind. Even if not landing, it is worth taking Puffin Sound in suitable conditions if you have AC2125. Halftide Rock in the middle of the channel shows towards LW, making the passage on the west side straightforward.

Portmagee Channel from SW

Valentia Island

Valentia River

Visitors' moorings

Portmagee Quay

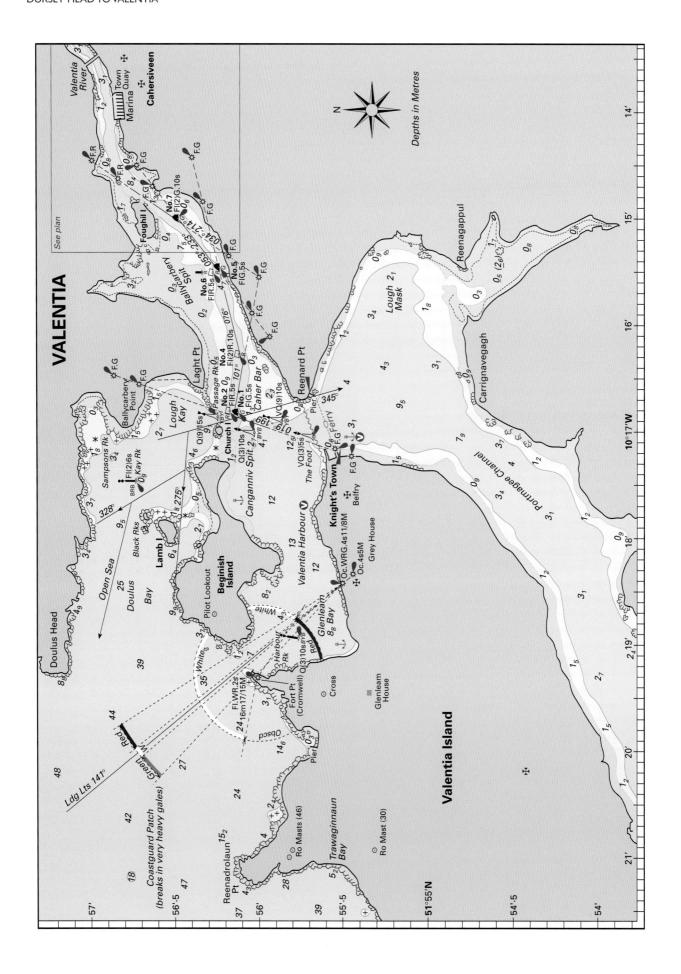

VALENTIA

The entrance to Portmagee can be very rough with violent gusts, but in fair weather the pilotage is simple using AC2125 or the plan on C56. As the channel narrows at Reencaheragh Point there is a reef to starboard and rocky islands to port. Now head ESE towards the anchorage on the chart until Quay Brack is abeam to port. The bay to starboard is an excellent anchorage clear of busy Skelligs traffic and currents. Sound in to the middle, off a little quay on the mainland. To proceed to the harbour turn ENE parallel and close to the north shore; there are rocks to starboard. Ahead will be yellow visitors' moorings in a small bay. Keep these to port before turning towards the pier in the, now deep, central channel. There is an underwater cable to the island just west of the pier but it is possible to anchor just below the bridge. Anchor on the north side to avoid the worst of the currents and to give fishing vessels room to manoeuvre. It is very peaceful here and is close to the town quay or the pontoon below the Skelligs Experience. Using the tender from the visitors' moorings expect much wash from speeding Skelligs' boats.

Water and fish ice are available on the quay. By the bridge there is a bottle and can bank with limited rubbish disposal. There are food shops, nice pubs and restaurants. The Moorings, a small hotel, offers yachtsmen showers when rooms change occupancy in the mornings; arrange this the evening before. The Fishermen's Bar does traditional Irish meals and is popular with locals. To visit the Skelligs go with Des Lavelle from his pontoon at the Skellig Experience. Turf (never peat) harvesting can be seen a short distance along the Cahersiveen road. Finally, do not miss Portmagee's award-winning public lavatories; the Gents has a slab of black Valentia slate which is difficult to miss. There is good accommodation for cruise followers, convenient for exploring Valentia Island, at The Moorings ☎ 066 947 7108 *Email* moorings@iol.ie

Potmagee's award-winning facilities

VALENTIA ISLAND

Valentia (pronounced 'Valencha') has nothing to do with Spain; the derivation is from the Gaelic 'Béal Inis' – island in the river mouth. For boats which can pass under the bridge it is only 4 miles to Valentia Harbour along the Portmagee Channel. With moderate draught this is easier at LW. The least sounding, albeit made in 1849, is 1.5m between the perches which mark the first half-mile to the bend. Then it is a clear run to the harbour. The chart shows 3m just beyond the bridge where a deep-draught boat, having negotiated the bridge at LW, could await the tide. Halfway along the channel is an excellent boatyard (Murphy Marine Services ☎ 087 280 9861) which can lift a 20-tonne boat.

In 1867 the original Valentia Observatory was built on Reenaloughan Point, utilising the new electric telegraph to transmit weather observations. Meteorological observations had been instigated by Post Captain (later

Looking towards the main NW entrance to Valentia Harbour at LW

The old Observatory
Des Lavelle

Admiral) Fitzroy, Hydrographer to the Royal Navy, much earlier. The Observatory was relocated to Cahersiveen in 1892. This has recently been superseded by a modern observatory; the Victorian building is being renovated. It contains fascinating meteorological, seismological and other instruments, with viewing only by appointment. For a very full history, search the web for 'Valentia Observatory'.

VALENTIA HARBOUR VIA THE MAIN NORTHWEST ENTRANCE

For tall-masted vessels it is 8 miles from Portmagee to the main entrance to Valentia Harbour. The signal tower on Bray Head is well-preserved, unlike the cliffs below. From Bray Head the 13-mile area of open water to the north is the widest in this guide. The Blasket Islands lie to the west of Mount Eagle and Brandon Mountain. Valentia's cliffs have many rock slides and the finger of slate shown on the chart east of Echala Rocks is no more. Rounding Beenaryaka Head all of the Dingle's feminine curves, and the surf off Castlemain, come into view. Low cliffs are of black slate topped by unstable boulders and shale. The masts of Valentia Radio lie ahead on Geokaun Hill, down which tumbles the waste from the famous slate quarry. The stone is relatively soft. It was not split, but cut by long 'saws' using flints, imported as ballast, for the cutting medium. The flat slabs were used in the best billiard tables and were easily worked to make ornamental fireplaces and so on. Slate is again being quarried, in a small way, and worked in Knight's Town. The quarry, tunnelled right through the hillside, and the works, should be visited.

Seine fishing with pulling boats was once a great industry, operated from many small harbours around West Cork and West Kerry. A 'six-oar boat' raced with a 13-man crew, is still a stirring site at the many regattas. Trawaginnaun Bay, just west of the approach, outside Fort Point lighthouse, was a seine-boat harbour. On a calm hot June afternoon *Balair* anchored there outside many rocks. A few minutes later a thick mist drifted in from the sea. This dispersed over the warm land, but it shows how fickle Irish mist can be. The old pier is in good condition with landing steps. Just west of the pier are the footprints, preserved in slate, of one of the first sea-creatures to develop limbs and live on land, 370 million years ago. This is known as the Tetrapod Trackway. Later, just along the coast, Valentia MRSC and CGR station was visited. The radio officers you have been talking to via remote aerials since leaving Cork are very welcoming; they seldom get visited by yachtsmen.

VALENTIA HARBOUR PILOTAGE

Tides HW Cóbh –0100, with on average 0.5m less water
Tides run simultaneously into Portmagee at up to 1kn and from the north at 1½kn, meeting in the Portmagee channel
RNLI Offshore Severn

ICP and ISDs mention a magnetic anomaly in the vicinity of The Blaskets. But calculating the current variation from the compass roses on AC2125 (Valentia) gives an error of 03°W. The UK Hydrographic Office states that the correct variation for Valentia in 2005 was 06°38′W, with an annual rate of change of 10′E. See also Magnetic Variation under Pilotage and Navigation in *Introduction*.

There are two northerly entrances (one for small craft) into this well-sheltered harbour, and into the Valentia River for Cahersiveen Marina. Both entrances can be dangerous in heavy weather from the northwest.

MAIN NW ENTRANCE

Entrance is straightforward, though the incorrect variation used did not help in picking up the 141° leading line. By day the front mark is a large white cone with vertical red stripes; the rear a red upright arrow on a white wall. These have occulting lights – the front directional. The narrow entrance is between Beginish Island and Fort (Cromwell) Point lighthouse. The lighthouse has a red sector covering Harbour Rock, which has a lit ECM, just inside the entrance. At night it is best to anchor south of Harbour Rock. There is a lovely anchorage off the beach in Glenleam Bay with a few moorings close in. There are visitors' moorings to the west and south of The Foot, a shallow spit off Knight's Town with a lit ECM. The southeast facing

bay of Beginish Island has an anchorage. Land on the long strand to explore this interesting island or to view the tricky entrance to the Valentia River.

Alternative entrance for small craft

This entrance, from Doulus Bay then through Lough Kay, was unmarked in 2004. However, with the new marina at Cahersiveen it was considered necessary to put in navigational marks for visitors. These were being laid when we went to press, but exact positions and lights of an Isolated Danger Mark for Kay Rock, a WCM guarding Passage Rock and two cardinals for negotiating Caher Bar had not been officially promulgated. Additional lateral marks for the passage up river to the marina are also being laid. All this is shown (August 2005) on a hand drawn approach plan in www.yachtcharterkerry. com. The plans onthese pages are based on this and on the visual transits through Lough Kay in ISDs.

The best contact for the latest information is Andrew Cooke who charters a Moody 31 with plans for a 40-foot yacht from Cahersiveen Marina. He liaises with Kerry County Council (the harbour authority) over the new and improved marks for Doulus Bay and upriver to the marina.

Andrew Cooke ☎ 066 947 2244
*Email*andrew@qcbar.com
www.yachtcharterkerry.com

Yacht Charter

See *Appendix*

VALENTIA HARBOUR AND KNIGHT'S TOWN

This is seldom used by commercial shipping now. But in 1865 the world's largest ship, *The Great Eastern*, operated out of the port to lay the first transatlantic cable, terminating in Newfoundland. The cable went sub-marine at the western end of Portmagee Channel in Fouilhomurrum Bay, with later cables laid out of Waterville and Ballinskelligs.

Knight's Town is named after the Knights of Kerry (the FitzGeralds) who were benign and beloved (both unusual) Protestant landlords. They lived locally (again unusual) and their old residence (Glenleam) has a

Balair **anchored below the bridge at Portmagee. The black object on the pulpit is a Danforth anchor, with half a tyre to protect sail**

Tetrapod footprints
Des Lavelle

The Transatlantic Cable Station in Knight's Town, Valentia

beautiful garden open to the public. Knight's Town museum gives the full history of the trials and final triumph of laying the first Atlantic Telegraph Cable, and much else. Read *Valentia. A Different Irish Island* by Nellie O'Cleirigh before exploring further with OSI 83. Near the conspicuous white buildings of the Atlantic Telegraph Company in Knight's Town is the Altazamuth Stone. Here, at the end of a baseline extending to Russia, the longitude of Valentia was calculated, by triangulation and astronomical readings, in 1862. Marconi had another experimental radio station near the Coast Guard Radio aerials on Reenadrolaun Point.

Knight's Town has a hotel, PO and store. The Fuchsia is excellent. Catherine and Tom Healy serve Irish as well as international food. Their restaurant's name sake flourishes in Ivernia. An import from South America, it flowers too late to set seed but rampages everywhere by vegetative means.

IRISH FISH CHOWDER

With thanks to Tom and Catherine of The Fuchsia Restaurant, Valentia, on whose recipe this is based.

Ingredients for 4
1½–2lbs selected fish, fresh or smoked, e.g. salmon, cod, halibut, smoked haddock, monkfish, hake, cubed or sliced
1–2oz each of prawns, mussels and shrimps

To cook
Make a stock of fish bones and skins, boiled in lightly salted water to cover. Place fish in a large pan, keeping the shellfish aside, with enough stock to just cover the fish. Add a glass of white wine and cook on moderate heat until fish is tender – about 15 minutes.

The Sauce
A carrot, leek, celery stalk, fresh herbs and 2–3 garlic segments, all finely chopped and cooked in 1tbsp best oil until soft. Add a small tin of chopped tomatoes or 2 large ripe tomatoes, skinned, chopped and cooked until soft, and a small amount of tomato purée. Heat, then stir gently into fish with the shellfish and cook for a further few minutes.
Serve with slices of Irish Soda Bread and fresh Kerry butter, or hot new potatoes.

It is possible to berth across the end of the main pier, where there is water, but the ferry to Reenard Point for Cahersiveen berths on the outside of this pier at night. This shuttling ferry is always busy and it should be possible to get a lift into Cahersiveen and back. At Reenard Point, O'Neil's Seafood Bar is excellent. Ice can be obtained from nearby Kerry Wild Salmon who have an excellent shop in Cahersiveen.

UPSTREAM TO CAHERSIVEEN

See page 131 regarding proposed marks. The transits (2005) published on charts, in ISDs and the almanac are almost obsolete, though some new lateral buoys have been installed. The faded yellow bands on the transit poles are to have day glow paint and the lights made more powerful. Some of the poles are obscured by trees, notably those for the 078° transit. Start upstream as soon as there is suffcient water over the Caher Barn. Near low water currents show this well. *Balair* had no problem in good visibility, though few of the transits came in soon enough. It was more important to study the chart than run aground searching for them. An extra hand with binoculars would have been a great help. The red post on Ballycarberry Spit is conspicuous. Track from this on 053° until the east side of Foughil Island bears 034°, then keep close to this island. In 2004 there were new lateral buoys ahead, though these were not aligned with the transit. Approaching the front leading mark on Daniel's Rock on the 034° transit do not turn for the SHMs off the bend to starboard too soon. These mark a drying mud bank.

CAHERSIVEEN MARINA

This is the place for a thorough rest, showers and to revictual. It has a chair lift for diabled sailors. In 2004 the narrow entrance, with strong cross currents and a sharp turn after entering, was tricky for larger yachts. This entrance may be improved. The long riverside pontoon can be used to await slack water. The temporary shore-side facilities were adequate, but new marina buildings are going up now, with a diesel berth planned. At present, green diesel is from a tank ashore. Rubbish disposal was not adequate but there is a bottle and can bank on the way into town.

This marina was conceived, and is owned, by a consortium of local business people keen to attract cruising and local sailors to what was a thriving fishing and agricultural market

Looking up the Valentia River towards Cahersiveen at LW

town. What they planned will be achieved. Some other harbours in Cork and Kerry have mooted marinas for years but boating folk still wait.

Town Quay

This is just above the marina; a concrete and gravel slip separates the two. Timber was exported from here until 1980. It has 2.5m to 3m and it is possible to go alongside by steps, but beware of the truncated slip (shown in the

photograph on the following page). There is a water tap.

CAHERSIVEEN

It is a short walk into 'Sive', as Carhersiveen is known. This has all shops, and an excellent hardware store sells Gaz. Good Centra and Spar supermarkets make it unnecessary to travel to a small, out-of-town, SuperValu.

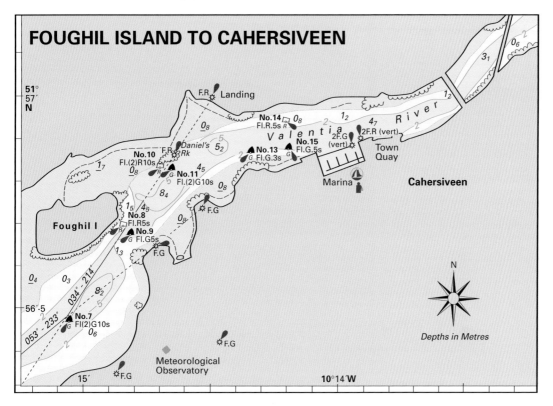

Truncated slip
Town Quay (water)
New houses to be built
Beach for drying out
Temporary marina building
Narrow entrance
SHM
SHM

Cahersiveen Marina at LW in summer 2004

Sive's tourist office is good. Get *The O'Connell Heritage Trail* there. Daniel O'Connell was born here; his parents' tomb is in the ruined Abbey of the Holy Cross. The trail is an excellent guide to all of interest within walking or cycling distance, with comprehensive information on all the places mentioned. To complement this, visit the restored Royal Irish Constabulary Barracks. Naturally this was fired in 1922 but has been fully restored as an exhibition centre, with much additional information on Sive. Ballycarbery Castle, two stone forts and the lovely bathing harbour of Cuas Crom (Cooncrome on the map) are within easy cycling distance, as is a disused turf-fired power station at the mouth of the River Fearta.

Seine boats competing in a regatta go downstream past Cahersiveen Marina

Mike Murts in Cahersiveen advertises 'Everything from a needle to an anchor'

As *Balair* spent 18 days in Valentia and Sive (mostly holed up by the southwesterly gales of June 2004), there are three other restaurants to be recommended. QC's seafood bar and restaurant is excellent. Andrew Cooke and his wife, Kate, run this and also 10° West Yacht Charter, so it is a good meeting place for sailors. For traditional Irish food, try the Town House pub. Nearest to the marina, for a before-supper stout and a check on the TV isobars, is the old railway hotel – now the Daniel O'Connell. This does evening meals and a roast lunch every day. Mike Murts is a traditional Irish bar which claims to sell 'everything from a needle to an anchor'. The website www.cahersiveen.info has much more via 'links'.

The Royal Irish Constabulary Barracks at Cahersiveen. Fired in 1922, they have been restored by the consortium that built the marina

5 VALENTIA TO TRALEE

The Blasket Islands. A yacht sails south out of Blasket Sound, between Dunmore Head and Great Blasket Island, with Inishtooskert in the distance

5 VALENTIA TO TRALEE

Ports, harbours and anchorages
Kells Bay – Dingle Harbour and
Marina – Ventry Bay –
Great Blasket Island
Smerwick Harbour – Brandon –
Scraggane Bay – Fenit Marina –
Barrow Harbour

Arrival ports
Valentia (Cahersiveen Marina)
Dingle (Marina)
Tralee (Fenit Marina)

Charts and maps
Passage and planning charts
Imray C56 & C57 or AC 2254
Useful large-scale charts
AC 2790, 2739
OSI Discovery Series maps 83, 70, 71

Coastguard radio MRSC and relay station with working channels
Valentia MRSC VHF 23,
MF 1752kHz
Shannon Ch 28

RNLI Lifeboats
Valentia, Fenit

Important landfall lights
Great Skellig,
Fort (Cromwell) Point
Iniskteeraght
Loop Head
Little Samphire Island

Tourist information
Cork Kerry Tourism, Aras Fáilte,
Grand Parade, Cork
☎ 021 4273251 *Fax* 021 4273504
Email info@corkkerrytourism.ie
www.ireland.travel.ie
www.dingle-peninsula.ie

A BRIEF DESCRIPTION OF THE AREA

The Dingle Peninsula, also known as
Corcaguiney, bisects this area. Apart from
Valentia, Dingle Bay has no islands and is
relatively wider than the other rias. The
southern shores, along the Iveragh ('Eev-rah')
Peninsula, have only one small haven east of
Valentia suitable for yachts. This is lovely
Kells Bay, at the western end of the mighty
Knocknadobar Range. Kells has visitors'
moorings and an anchorage protected from
the Atlantic swell, which can break in fury on
the sand hills which now almost cut off the
silted harbour of Castlemaine. Castlemaine is
no place for yachts, though a large new quay
for the shellfish vessels which work this huge
mainly drying lagoon has been built recently.

The northern shore is the mountainous
Dingle Peninsula. This has just two safe
havens; almost land-locked Dingle and large
Ventry Harbour which is open to the
southeast. The now-uninhabited Blasket
Islands lie off Mount Eagle at Corcaguiney's
western end. Northward from these most
westerly islands of the British Isles, said a
local sailor, the wilder coasts of Ireland really
start. But do not let this deter you. As *Balair*
did, wait in Dingle or Ventry Harbours for
suitable conditions before sailing north, or in
Fenit or Smerwick Harbour if southbound.

Dingle is a lovely town, despite the tourists
of high summer. From here or Ventry it is not
a great distance to walk or cycle to Smerwick

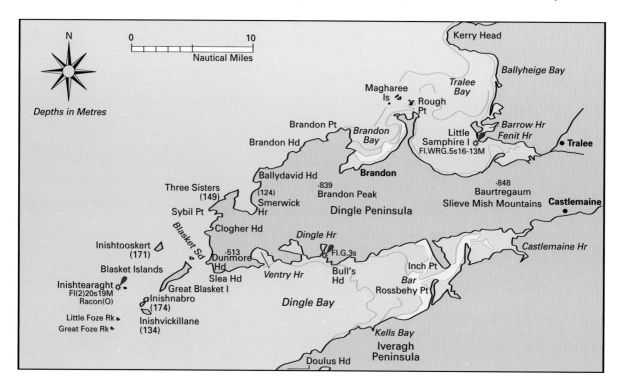

Harbour, the lovely north-facing natural harbour featured on the cover. From Smerwick eastwards are to be found some of the most important antiquities of Southwest Ireland.

Coasting east from Smerwick the cliffs are the wildest and most dramatic of Cork or Kerry, until reaching sheltered (from the west) Brandon Bay. This has a good anchorage off the quays of pretty Brandon. Entering relatively shallow Tralee Bay, sandstone gives way to the limestone which comprises three-quarters of the rest of Ireland. Fenit ('Feenit'), with its marina, has become the port for Tralee. Tralee is the administrative capital of County Kerry and has the most varied shopping since Cork. This once great trading port has excellent communications by road, rail, air and from Fenit.

Fenit Marina makes an excellent first arrival for a visitor but is not convenient for major victualling. At present this means a road journey of 13km to Tralee, with a bus service limited to Wednesdays and Fridays. Fenit and Tralee get a full description at the end of this section, which starts with departure from Valentia, a good arrival port which is covered in Section 4. Dingle, with its marina, is the best arrival port.

Each arrival port is sufficiently lit for a night arrival, though Tralee Bay off Fenit has several small unlit rocks and islands. Little Samphire Island lighthouse shows a safe sector through these.

VALENTIA TO DINGLE VIA KELLS

Should the new marks (see page 131) not be in place it is best to describe the passage for small craft into and out of Valentia in this section. This was *Balair*'s departure in good visibility; it is suggested that visitors initially take this outbound route, as it starts from identified marks. The first is Reenard Point (the mainland ferry terminal). Plot the provisional tracks shown on the plan on your large scale chart. Clear of Caher Bar get on a back bearing of about 345° from Reenard, keeping close to Church Island with drying Passage Rock well to starboard – a WCM is planned to show the safe water here. Stay on this transit until Lamb Island is about to close with the north side of Beginish Island, turning on to this transit of about 275°. When Reenard Point is just open of the northeast corner of Beginish turn on to this transit of about 328°, to pass between drying Kay Rock (to get an Isolated Danger Mark) and Black Rocks. Proceed on 328° until 2 cables north of Black Rocks before turning for the open

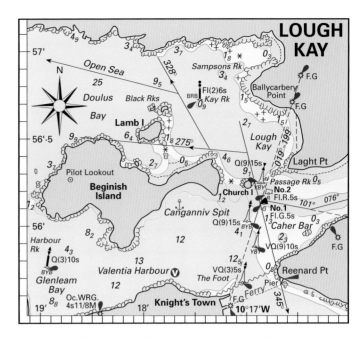

sea. In fair conditions this was all straightforward, with not a murmur from Joy!

There was plenty of time to admire the scenery. Crews of boats anchored off Beginish sunbathed on the pebble beach. To starboard, citizens of Cahersiveen were enjoying the sun on White Strand. Beyond them unspoilt farmland rose towards the summit of Castlequin. Ahead The Blaskets, with some notable stacks, gradually opened beyond Doulus Head with its stone cairn. The head was festooned with ropes and rock climbers; many pot buoys lay below cliffs which resembled slabs of melting black chocolate.

Balair's en route destination was pretty Kells Bay, nine miles east of Doulus. Rounded hills at first sloped to less eroded low cliffs, with inlets to the seine fishing *cuans* (harbours) of Cooncrome and Coonana. Their piers are very popular with swimmers from nearby Cahersiveen. Both *cuans* widen to the northwest into day anchorages, though *Balair* had no time to sample these. The chart indicates a bottom of sand, mud and shells with a flood along the coast of ½kn. HW Valentia is about Cóbh –0100 with, on average, 0.5m less water.

To the north, the Dingle has a much smoother and more feminine form than rugged Iveragh. Even in a stable air mass, warm air from the sea clothed its mountains with cumulus which, though topped with lenticular cloud, gave heavy showers. The warm air was then drawn into a leeward valley to fill it with mist. The peninsula protecting Dingle Harbour looked like a large island, with Brandon's peaks thrusting bosom-like beyond. The head of Dingle Bay was a mass of distant breakers on the dunes of Inch and Rossbehy Points.

Anchorage Visitors' moorings

Kells Bay

Kells Bay from anchorage outside local moorings. Note yellow visitors' mooring

KELLS BAY

Intimate Kells Bay, southwest from Dingle, was another *cuan*. Approaching from the west the bay is hidden until it opens up behind a low sheltering headland. Visitors' moorings are just behind the point, off a reef, with space to anchor in 9m outside local moorings. The anchor held well and came in clean but it was too deep to check for weed. Gusts are probable with a strong southwesterly from adjacent high ground. With a small beach, a pier, a few holiday homes and discreet caravans this is a select holiday resort. A solitary cottage with a slip and boathouse has been modernised.

On a long holiday weekend families were out fishing for breakfast and later exploring the low rocky shores from small beaches. About 15 minutes' walk along the road to Castlemaine there is a filling station and store. Further on, the graceful Gleenisk Viaduct carried the disused railway to Cahersiveen over a deep valley. OSI 70 just shows this and a large waterfall. This map will also be needed for west Corcaguiney.

DINGLE

Large but shallow Dingle Harbour, with a well-marked dredged channel to the marina, is 9 miles to the northwest of Kells. To the east, Dingle Bay again indicates – from soundings and the shores – that it was once another vast estuary. If arriving from Dingle, Kells lies between two hills. Closing the bay water is still just visible between Great Blasket and the mainland.

At night the only aid for the 1½ cable wide narrows leading into Dingle is a small light tower to starboard, with the first channel marks ahead, on a track of 320°. (Precise navigation is given below.) Outside to port there are some nasty rocks. On the mainland beyond these is the stone Esk Tower, a day mark with finger board directing vessels towards the harbour entrance. The main daytime hazard is tourist-laden boats chasing after the harbour's famous dolphin. It seems sad that this fine creature has to be harried thus, but Fungie seems to enjoy bringing additional euros into Dingle.

On the final approach, Dingle, with its many new houses on each side of the port, does not look the very attractive 18th-century town that it is. Do not call ahead for a berth unless you have a very large boat. Berthing Master Johnny Murphy (☎ 087 232844), or harbourmaster Lt Cdr Brian Farrel – a keen yachtsman – will direct you initially to an outer pontoon. (There is plenty of room to manoeuvre whilst preparing to go alongside – with at least 5m of water.) Brian welcomes a visit from yachtsmen to his office. Later Johnny will bring diesel, if needed, in his or your cans. Marina an Daingin (www.dinglemarina.com) has excellent modern facilities, shared with a dive school, and a good slip.

For limited chandlery, ferry bookings and much else, visit Dingle Marine & Leisure at the marina. The smart passenger ferry *Peig Sayers* runs regular excursions to Great Blasket Island. Another ferry takes up to 12 passengers, with bicycles, to Valentia in 40 minutes. From Reenard Point they can visit Knight's Town, the Skelligs or go into Cahersiveen.

In Dingle harbour you may see your first curragh ('curruck'); in Gaelic the name is *naombóg* ('ny-vog' with a long 'o'). Covered with heavy tarred canvas on a wooden frame, these were in common use to convey people and domestic animals over the bouncy waters around western Corcaguiney. Drawing little water, they are easy to get aboard without a soaking. They are remarkably resilient alongside the many rocky landings and are very manoeuvrable, with just rounded-off square oars in fixed thole pins. When practising for regattas they move at high speed.

DINGLE

This was (and still is) an important market town and fishing port, but tourism has become a major summer industry. A large SuperValu is close to the adjoining harbour for fishing vessels. Having revictualled, with tourists thronging the harbour-side streets, you may feel this is not the place to be. When you have obtained a good map of the town from the helpful Tourist Office, and explored

Dingle Harbour from S. Mount Brandon is in top right corner

Three Sisters

Light tower

White patch

**Dingle Marina
from N**

**Foxy John's in
Main Street,
Dingle**

old Dingle – preferably before breakfast – you will think otherwise. Go up Green Street from SuperValu, noting Dick Mac's – with the names of the cast of *Ryan's Daughter* set in the pavement. Later you will meet mainly local folk there, drinking in what was once also a shoe shop. (In 1969 Robert Mitchum astounded locals with his capacity for stout.) When you arrive in lovely Main Street seek out Foxy John's hardware shop. He will sell you a Guinness and you can hire a bike. A good pub for *craic* is An Droichead Beag at the bottom of this street. The book shop is An Café Liteaartha, where you can also browse the papers with a snack and tea or coffee. It sells the well-known books by Blasket Islanders, such as *An Old Woman's Reflections* by Peig Sayers. For the full story of these now-deserted islands read Joan and Ray Stagles *The Blasket Islands*. For very full information on the Dingle and its history www.dingle-peninsula.ie is excellent.

DINGLE PILOTAGE

Tides Cóbh –0055

Approaching from the southwest the light tower at the cable-wide entrance, inside Beenbane Point, just open of Reenbeg Point clears dangerous rocks to port by two cables. There is no leading line so position to the south of the light tower to bring the first of the channel marks (they all have lights) on to about 320°. A patch of white paint on the cliff opposite the light tower serves as a mark in poor visibility. Past the first SHM off Black Point the channel is dredged to 2.6m and is 40m wide. The plan shows the marked channel into the marina and fishing harbour. Heading north up the channel, leading marks astern – with black and white diamonds and occulting lights – align on a back bearing of 182°. The marina entrance is to port, marked by fixed red and green vertical lights. The deep pool south of the bend in the channel is now used by fishing vessels for keep-pots, but anchorage can be found in 3m northwest of the bend, southwest of the drying patch.

Main Street, Dingle

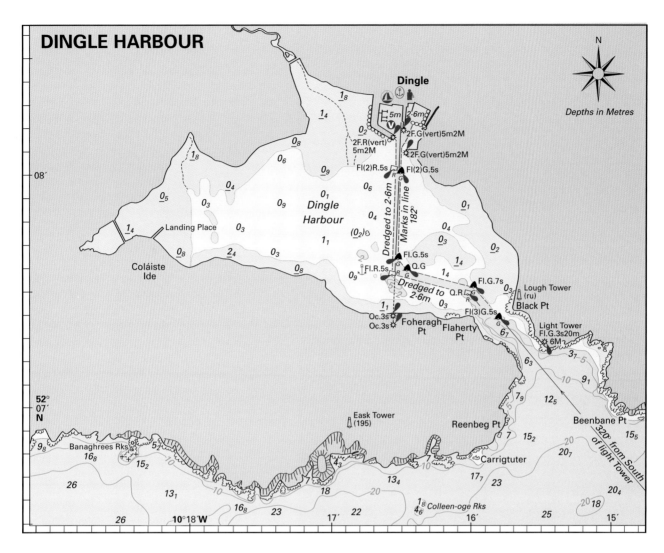

DINGLE HARBOUR

Dingle

N

Depths in Metres

2F.G(vert)5m2M
2F.G(vert)5m2M
Fl(2)G.5s
2F.R(vert) 5m2M
Fl(2)R.5s
Dredged to 2·6m
Marks in line 182°
Dingle Harbour
Fl.G.5s
Q.G
Fl.R.5s
Dredged to 2·6m
Q.R
Fl.G.7s
Lough Tower (ru)
Black Pt
Fl(3)G.5s
Landing Place
Coláiste Ide
Oc.3s
Oc.3s
Foheragh Pt
Flaherty Pt
Light Tower Fl.G.3s20m 6M
08′
52° 07′ N
Eask Tower (195)
Reenbeg Pt
Beenbane Pt
320° from South of light Tower
Banaghrees Rks
Carrigtuter
Colleen-oge Rks
10°18′W
17′
16′
15′

DINGLE TO VENTRY

Dingle to Ventry is a popular day sail. If taking the safe passage inside Colleen-oge Rocks keep well to starboard to allow opposite traffic to keep inside these rocks too. The near-vertical slates of the cliffs are all the colours of old red sandstone; horizontal crystalline layers look at first like roosting seabirds.

Three Sisters   Smerwick Harbour

Visitors' moorings

New quay and slip

Another store and pub

Slip

Ventry Harbour from S. Coon Pier is in the foreground. Ventry is on the right

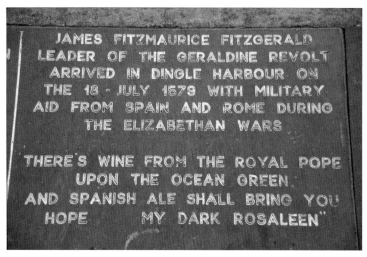

Stone plaque on Coon Pier in Ventry Harbour. The later Lord Ventry could not have approved!

Ventry village from the anchorage and visitors' moorings

VENTRY HARBOUR

There are no hazards entering Ventry Harbour except for a patch to starboard which sometime breaks. Visitors' moorings are near the new pier below Ventry Village. There are anchorages sheltered from all directions, but large patches of weed have to be avoided. If caught by a 'blow' anchor in at least 5m. The pier is lit at night for anchor bearings. A good slip is handy for landing bicycles. At high water it is possible to go alongside the pier. It has ladders and good tyings; a few fishing vessels use it for unloading but there is no fresh water.

Ventry has an excellent store with a post office. There is a pub and a restaurant. Do not use the holiday caravan site for rubbish disposal – past this are a refuse bin and bottle bank. An interesting pottery has a café serving all meals from breakfast to supper. Sunsets in the col between Mount Eagle and Croaghmarhin are superb, especially when horses from a local riding school gallop along the strand below. There is another pub and store by the chapel, on the west side of the harbour (see charts or OSI 70).

It is 7km by road to Dunquin, the mainland harbour for The Blaskets, with a good Visitor Centre. On the way there are beehive huts (*clochans*) and a museum near Dun Beg Fort. This is *Ryan's Daughter* country (34 years on she was wearing jeans with the obligatory bare midriff!). There are also good views of The Blaskets.

Smerwick Harbour has several of the best preserved historic sites in southwest Ireland. Should weather or time prevent a visit, it is only 6km away. The road is not steep and it passes the interesting castle at Rahinnane. Smerwick is about the same distance from Dingle but by a busy main road.

COON PIER

On the south side of Ventry Harbour, Coon Pier should be visited – anchored off, by foot or by bicycle. It is beautifully constructed and topped with slate with an interesting stone plaque detailing the history of Dingle. It has a slip. Once a base for seine fishing, this was Lord Ventry's main landing. He was a fervent early 19th-century advocate of Protestantism, but the Great Famine undid much of his efforts. He lived in a beautiful 18th-century mansion on his Burnham Estate, at the drying western end of Dingle Harbour. His house is now Coláiste Ide, a girls' boarding school.

Lord Ventry's mansion, now a girls' boarding school, at western end of Dingle Harbour

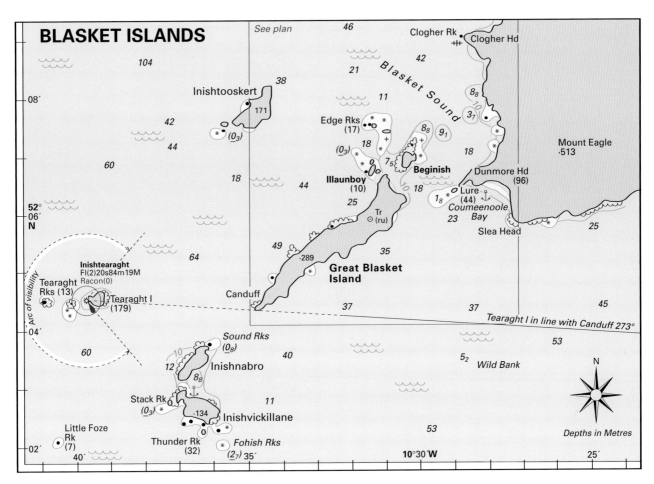

BLASKET ISLANDS

See plan

Depths in Metres

10°30′W

(map labels:)
104
Inishtooskert 38
171
(0₃)
42
44
60
18
64
Inishtearaght
Fl(2)20s84m19M
Racon(0)
Tearaght Rks (13)
Tearaght I (179)
Arc of visibility
60
Sound Rks (0₈)
10
12
Inishnabro
8₈
Stack Rk (0₃)
Little Foze Rk (7)
Thunder Rk (32)
·134
Inishvickillane
0
Fohish Rks (2₇) 35′
40′
02′
04′
52° 06′ N
08′

46
Clogher Rk
Clogher Hd
42
21
11
Blasket Sound
8₈
10
3₇
Edge Rks (17)
8₈ 9₁
(0₃)
18
7₅
Beginish
18
Illaunboy (10)
25
18
Dunmore Hd (96)
Mount Eagle ·513
1₈ Lure (44)
Coumeenoole Bay
23
Slea Head
25
Tr (ru)
49
·289
35
Great Blasket Island
Canduff
37
37
45
Tearaght I in line with Canduff 273°
53
40
5₂ Wild Bank
53
25′

1½km away, in the eastern corner of Ventry Harbour Lord Ventry had a deep-water quay in a narrow creek – a mile and a half from Coon Pier. This landing, south of Ballymore Point, would be ideal for a visit to the house, with its seven Ogham Stones and an excellent riding school.

THROUGH BLASKET SOUND FOR SMERWICK HARBOUR

Tidal streams in Blasket Sound
N-going (up to 3kn) begins HW Cóbh +0430
S-going begins HW Cóbh –0155
Up to 4kn between islands

In July, after days of mist and low cloud at Ventry, *Balair* was able to plan for the Blasket Sound near neaps and with the stream. In a light southwesterly it was a little lumpy off Dunmore Head and Sybil Point. The moderate Atlantic swell was the main culprit. There is a waiting anchorage in the bay between Slea and Dunmore Heads (see plan). The transit for the sound (015°) is the tower on Sybil Point on with pointed Clogher Rock. The worst seas can be expected off the reefs southwest of Dunmore Head and again approaching Clogher Head. It is safe to head west and north of the transit before the overfalls south of Clogher Head.

Coming from the south beware of Barrack Rock, 2½ miles southeast of Inishvickillane,

though this only breaks in gales. On track from Valentia Wild Bank (3 miles south of Dunmore Head) can have overfalls.

After Ventry the Slea Head Drive clings to the coast from Dunbeg to Dunquin; apart from coaches the steep hillsides are unspoilt. With binoculars scan for *clochans* amongst the sheep and stone walls. Great Blasket Island has an almost natural harbour, between two reefs, but landing is only by inflatable or from a curragh. Just to the north is a yellow mooring which yachts may share with the ferries, or they can anchor off the strand. This is a good spot just to view the only village of An Blascaod Mór, which was

The Three Sisters and the Brandon range from off Sybil Point

BLASKET SOUND

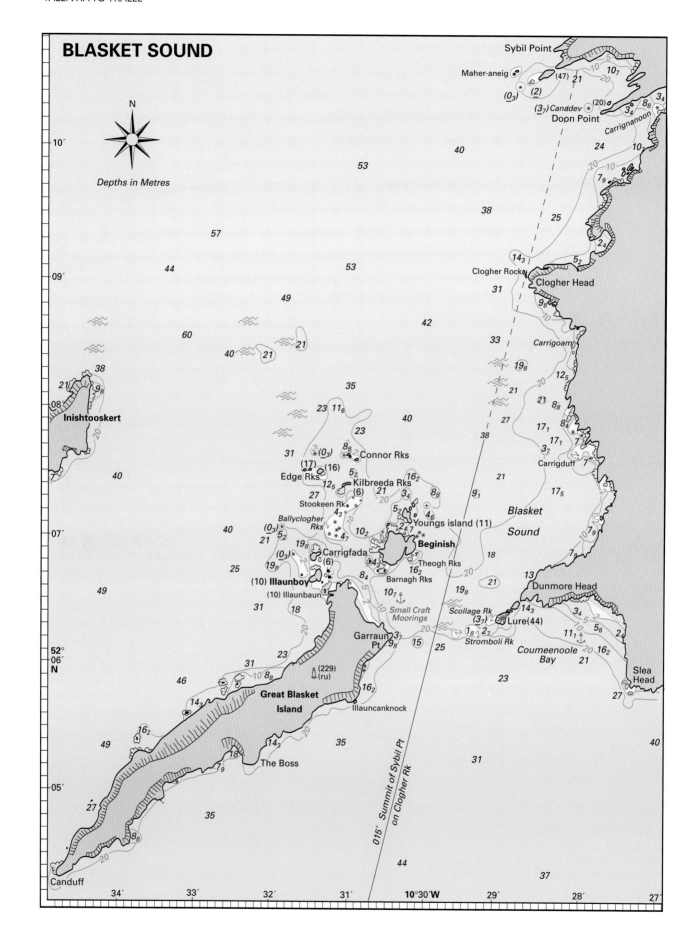

N

Depths in Metres

Sybil Point

Maher-aneig

(47) 21 10₇ 10₇
20

(0₃) (2)

(3₇) Canadev (20) 3₄ 8₈ 3₄

Doon Point

Carrignanoon

40 24 10

38 25 20 10

53 7₉

57 20

14₃

44 Clogher Rock

53 31 Clogher Head

49 9₈ 20

60 33 Carrigoam

40 21 19₈ 12₅ 21

35 40 27 8₈

23 11₆ 21 17₁ 8₄

38 23 3₇ 17₁ 7

Inishtooskert

31 (0₃) 8₈ Connor Rks 21 Carrigduff 7

(17) (16) 5₂ 16₂ 17₅

Edge Rks 12₅ Kilbreeda Rks 21 9₁ Blasket

27 (6) 3₄ Sound

Stookeen Rk 4₃ 8₈

4₃ 5₂ 18

Ballyclogher 4₆ Youngs island (11)

(0₃) Rks 10₂ 2₄ 7 7₉

21 5₂ ✱✱ Beginish

19₈ (0₃) 7₉

Carrigfada Theogh Rks 13

25 (6) 8₄ 16₂ Dunmore Head

(10) Illaunboy Barnagh Rks 14₃ 3₄ 5₆ 2₄

(10) Illaunbaun Scollage Rk (3₇) Lure(44) 11₁ 5 16₂

49 18 10₇ Small Craft 11₁ 2₄

31 Moorings 19₈ (1₈) 2₇ 21 Slea

23 Garraun 3₇ Stromboli Rk Coumeenoole Head

46 Pt 9₈ 15 25 Bay 21 27

14₃ (229) 40

16₂ Great Blasket 16₂ 23 31

Island Illauncanknock

49 14₃ 35

18 The Boss

27 ₇₉ 44 37

35 35

8₈

20

Canduff

34' 33' 32' 31' 10°30'W 29' 28' 27'

Deserted
village

Landing
place

Mooring for
ferries &
yachts

Anchorage
(clear of
ferries)

Boats wait off the landing place, below the deserted village on Great Blasket

finally abandoned in 1954. Now there are only summer homes. The most southwesterly island, Inishvickillane, is owned by a former Irish public figure. Beginish Island, which is left close to port, has ruined cottages and a flock of sheep. The sound may be busy with boats crossing to and from Dunquin.

After Clogher Head, the pointed Three Sisters rise northwestward above the now modern-looking village of Ballyferriter. This was the Blasket islanders' village for marriages, christenings and funerals. Much legend surrounds the Three Sisters, but in 1927 they were Lindbergh's landfall after his Atlantic crossing by air.

SMERWICK HARBOUR

After Sybil Point (a spike topped with a tower) the full majesty of the Three Sisters, with Brandon Mountain beyond, opens up. Smerwick Harbour is one of the most beautiful in all of Cork and Kerry. Beware of nets set on either side of the heads. Many amateur pots are set along the west side of the harbour. The plan shows a good anchorage just northeast of Dún an Óir. Holding is good in 6m abeam a small landing beach open to farmland above, leading to walks from the

Above
The southern entrance to Blasket Sound with Great Blasket Island in the distance

Below
The recently excavated monastic settlement near Riasc with the Three Sisters on the horizon

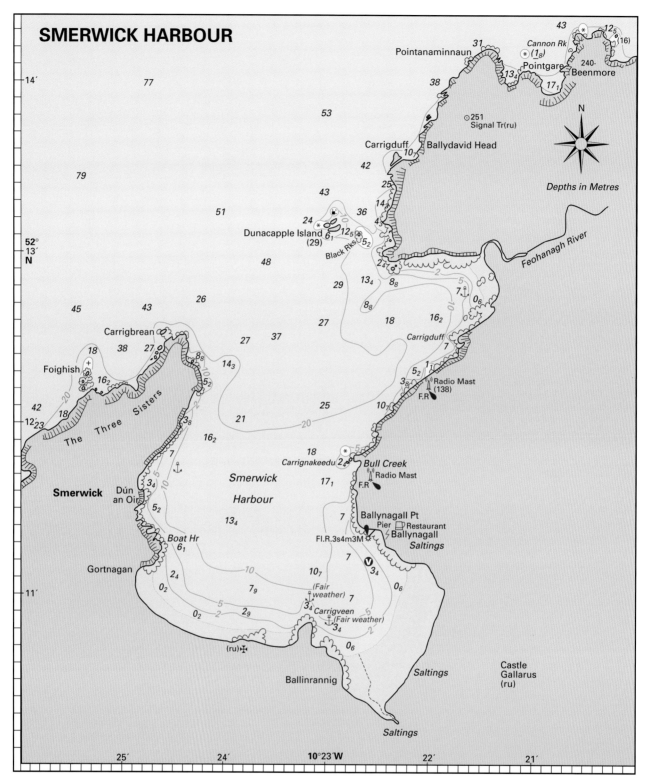

SMERWICK HARBOUR

Sisters to Sybil Head. Although this anchorage was sheltered from the wind there was a considerable swell out of the lee of the shore. About 4 cables to the south is a good boat-harbour with a slip. Do not confuse this with a ruined quay with a high-water slip, a boat-house and a modern house. From the boat-harbour it is 2km, partly along a normally safe bathing strand, to the shops, restaurants and pubs at Ballyferriter. It is a short walk to Dún an Óir (the fort of gold) from this landing. This was an Iron Age promontory fort. In 1580 it was re-fortified by 600 Spaniards and Italians, under Italian command, who had landed to support the revolt against English rule. Later an English fleet arrived in Smerwick, to be joined by Lord Grey and 800 soldiers. The Spanish and Italians surrendered but were beheaded and their heads thrown into the sea.

Despite this massacre, the south and east of Smerwick Harbour is the cradle of an early Christian civilisation dating from the late 6th and early 7th centuries. (Smerwick was originally a Viking settlement; the name comes from Norse words *smoer* and *wick*

Looking SE over the inner part of Smerwick Harbour. This is convenient for visiting the many ancient sites

The anchorage in Smerwick Harbour S of Ballydavid Head, looking NE towards the Brandon range of mountains

meaning 'butter harbour'.) Gallarus Oratory with its Visitor Centre, and nearby Kilmalkedar Church, get all the hype, but a far more interesting site, less frequented by tourists, is at An Riasc. This is easily reached from a good fair-weather anchorage, protected from swell, just east of another small boat-harbour with a slip south of Carrigveen (Tráigh an Fhiona on OSI 70). A road leads past holiday homes to Tigh Rhric – The Bridge Inn (you have been in the Gaeltacht since Dingle). Although developed for holidaymakers this is a general store selling groceries, home-made fare, fuel, petrol and diesel and with a restaurant and bar. Continue southeast from the inn and the next right leads to a recently-excavated monastic site with the remains of *clochans* and a boat-shaped oratory.

It was due to confusion with other Norse words that Ballydavid also became known as Ballynagall. This small fishing village has a

From the good anchorage just NW of Dún an Óir in Smerwick Harbour. Beware of pots along this shore!

Gallarus Oratory, near Ballydavid (Smerwick Harbour), was built about 1,300 years ago. The site has a visitors' centre

Ballydavid's new pier with slip in Smerwick Harbour. Besides having a 'flashing red' it is floodlit

long new pier, extending from rock into sand, with a slip and several ladders. This has a Fl.R light, it is floodlit and gives shelter from the swell and northwesterly winds. Yachts are welcome to come alongside to dry out. Kerry County Council installed AC but forgot to

connect taps on the water hydrant. There is a nice beach inside the pier, with a good pub and restaurant above. The village has a post office and small store. Visitors' moorings are to the southeast of the pier, some amongst fishing vessel moorings. Gallarus Oratory and the more interesting Kilmalkedar Church are within easy walking or cycling distance.

There is an attractive anchorage, with settled winds from the east but subject to swell, in the bay south of Ballydavid Head. A salmon river enters here and in mid-July a long string of buoys was set along the northern shores. (These could have been for salmon.) The Feohanagh River enters the head of the bay through a marsh, but Dooneen Pier, with nearby restaurant, is on the south side for a convenient landing. Do not sound too far in before anchoring as there are reefs, out to 4 metres, and possibly boulders. There are lovely walks from here, by road as far as Brandon Creek, where St Brendan is said to have set sail to discover America in a large sailing curragh. (See *The Brendan Voyage* by Tim Severin.) The energetic can take the Saints' Road to pay homage to St Brendan on Brandon Peak. At 952 metres this is Ireland's second highest mountain. This 'road' starts at Ballybrack (Baile Bhric on OSI 70), some 4km up the river valley. To get the most out of these walks, refer to Steve MacDonough's book (see *Appendix*) or click 'Feohanagh' on the Towns and Villages page of www.dingle-peninsula.ie

There are two well-lit radio masts north of Ballynagall (Ballydavid) for night bearings from any anchorage. One is for the dedicated FM frequency for RTE Radio. The only slight blight on Smerwick is the many new holiday homes scattered around the green hilly landscape, with its many sheep and mainly Kerry-cross cattle. To balance this are lovely views to the Blaskets and no 'Keep Out' signs.

SMERWICK TO FENIT

Give the rocks off the eastern entrance to Smerwick a good berth: they can break heavily. The coast from Ballydavid Head to Brandon Bay is like no other in Cork and Kerry. Ballydavid has a signal tower; just two vertical walls remain. The two headlands to the northeast could be the brothers of the Three Sisters. Brandon Creek has a few houses, then there is no modern building until Brandon Point. Brandon Mountain rises sheer from the sea. Past a landslide of red rock – where many streams cascade into the sea at 10°14′.5W – there are a few small stone enclosures (with a '*clochain*' – see OSI 70.) Just accessible from a curragh, was this St Brendan's secret garden? There is no coast road but at intervals manmade dividing boundaries slope steeply down to the cliffs. A few sheep cling to the slopes. These creatures suffer no vertigo, but sadly a white corpse sometimes lies on a ledge.

Sauce Creek is wild and rock-bound. Its name is an English corruption of the Irish *sás* (a trap). No flotsam can escape. Ahead, the high ground of Kerry Head rises island-like on the horizon. Pot buoys begin just before Deelick Point which has an old coastguard look-out. Brandon Point has a viewpoint and in the evening during the nesting season many Manx shearwaters home overhead to their broods. The point is accessible by road from Brandon in the bay around the corner.

BRANDON

This old village, with a stone pier curving around a beach, is very attractive. In the 19th century as many as a hundred curraghs fished from here. Salted mackerel were sent to North America; Kerry butter to Cork by sea and pack-horse. A few modern homes do not spoil its setting amongst gently sloping farm land. To the east a low sandy peninsula, with Magharee Islands off its tip, looks like a reef in some tropical sea.

For motor cruisers this is a popular evening run from Fenit. Yachts have ample room to anchor inside local moorings or off the attractive beach to the south. There is a store and the harbour-side pub does meals; for more sophisticated food there is another inn. Ask around for water. At Cloghane (4km) there is a store and two pubs.

On one of the last Sundays in August Brandon hosts a regatta, with teams of curraghs from all along the coast. You are still very much in the Gaeltach, so do not miss the Celtic festival of Lughnasa if you are there during the last weekend of July. This is a mixture of sheep shearing, dog trials, local food, poetry, music and dance.

The southwestern corner of Brandon Bay has many archaeological sites dating from the Bronze Age to early Christianity. Get information on all this, and maps of walks in the area, from the Visitor Centre in Cloghane. If you would rather catch brown trout take a fly rod to Cloghane's Owenmore River, but be prepared for the walk back to Brandon when the tide goes out.

FENIT MARINA VIA THE MAGHAREE ISLANDS

On track from Brandon the Magharee Islands do not justify their other name – the Seven Hogs – as initially there seem to be just three. The others appear to be attached to the peninsula of grass-covered sand. The tip of this and the islands are lumps of limestone. Use the plan and chart to make a visual passage through the Magharees for Fenit. In unsuitable weather route north of the Seven Hogs.

SCRAGGANE BAY

This has many fishing vessel moorings so it is best to anchor outside of these, though there is about 1m with swinging room just southeast of the pier. Beware of the reef of large boulders south of the pier. The piers and slip are much used for mooring and slipping large wooden lobster crates; and is also used by a dive school. The crates are also moored, almost submerged, amongst the fishing vessels. Nearly all the fishermen use curraghs

From the anchorage off Brandon looking NW

Cloghane   Brandon   Brandon
                                        Point

Pier

Scraggane
Bay

Looking W from Scraggane over Brandon Bay

Sunrise over Scraggane Bay. Note the many curraghs used as tenders

to reach their vessels. Walk to Fahamore, which has pubs and shops; across the peninsula you can see curraghs being built. There is a water tap on the pier outside a basic public lavatory which is cleaned daily. (This is true of most public lavatories in Cork

and Kerry away from the cities.) A 14ft standing stone, with a cross, stands in a field at Candiha, at the southern side of the bay.

It is possible to anchor, in 3 metres, off the side of the peninsula, south of fish farms. This is near Castlegregory which, as well as two small supermarkets and a post office, has a doctor and pharmacist. It is very popular with locals and tourists because of the miles of blue flag beaches for bathing and water sports. Nearby Lough Gill is a breeding place for the rare, and noisy, natterjack toad. These could disturb your sleep.

Illauntannig, the larger island across Magharee Sound, has a well-preserved monastery with two small oratories and three *clochans*. There is also a ruined church, a flock of sheep and a deserted farmhouse. Fresh water had to be collected from the mainland. In settled weather it is well worth a visit. An anchorage is shown on the plan; anchor according to draught and conditions east of the house and north of drying Thurran rock. Land on the beach.

MAGHAREES PILOTAGE

Tidal streas between Brandon and Tralee
E-going begin HW Cóbh +0550
W-going begin HW Cóbh –0035
These can be up to 3kn in Magharee Sound

Pilotage through the sound is straightforward in good visibility with a favourable tide. A transit marks the best water. This aligns the south side of The Rose (a conspicuous lump of an island off Fenit Island) with Fenit Castle and a church beyond on 106°, but these are not always easy to pick out. In this case there is a much better transit. Approaching from the west keep the north side of Gurrig Island astern on 280°, giving Illauntannig a reasonable berth. From the east Gurrig looks like a pan lid – flat with a knob in the middle. Keep it just open of Illauntannig on 280°. Tralee Bay is relatively shallow and two obstructions are on track to Fenit from the sound. They have been there since the days of Ireland's struggle for complete independence. If you do not like them, head east from the sound and pick up a suitable inbound bearing for Little Samphire Island lighthouse.

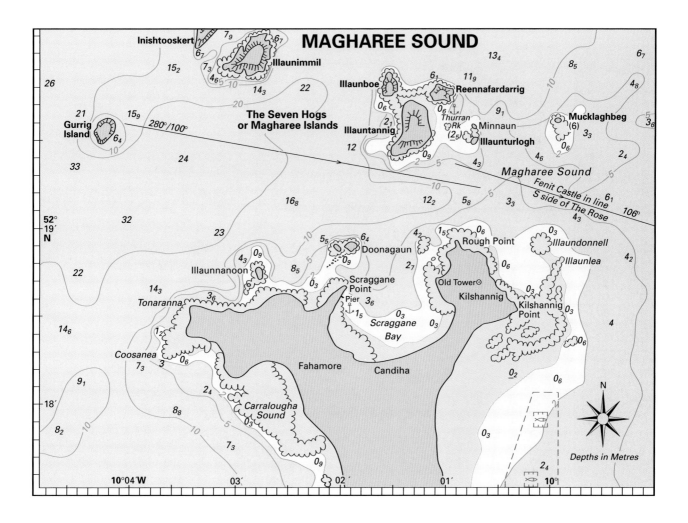

FENIT HARBOUR

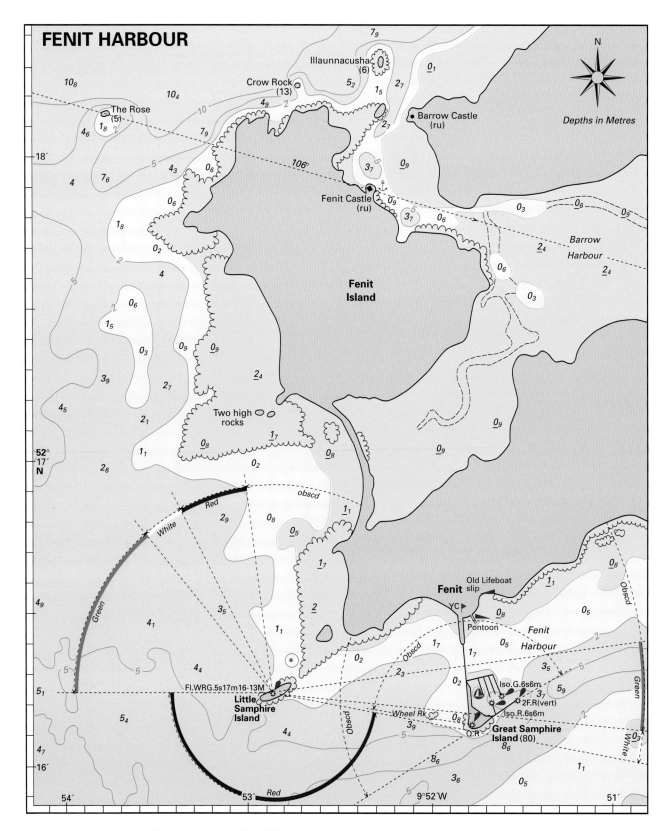

The Rose (5)

Crow Rock (13)

Illaunnacusha (6)

Barrow Castle (ru)

Depths in Metres

Fenit Castle (ru)

Barrow Harbour

Fenit Island

Two high rocks

obscd

Red

White

Green

FI.WRG.5s17m16-13M

Little Samphire Island

Wheel Rk

Obscd

Fenit YC

Old Lifeboat slip

Pontoon

Fenit Harbour

Iso.G.6s6m

2F.R(vert)

Iso.R.6s6m

Q.R

Great Samphire Island (80)

Green

White

Obscd

Red

9°52'W

FENIT HARBOUR AND MARINA

Tralee's original port was at Blennerville. In 1846 a ship canal was opened, extending from the town to three-quarters of a mile past Blennerville. In 1887, a long viaduct, carrying rail and road traffic, was built out to Great Samphire Island to accommodate larger vessels. This was extended to the east as a southern jetty to create Fenit harbour. Besides a commercial and fishing harbour there is now a marina protected by new moles to the north and east. An all-weather and an inshore RNLI lifeboat are based in the marina. Ships call regularly at the port, some to collect components for very large cranes built in Ireland. The marina has all the usual facilities. In 2004 the harbourmaster Michael O'Carrol and marina manager David Buttimore were very helpful.

Fenit Harbour and Marina looking E towards Tralee

FENIT PILOTAGE

Tides HW Cóbh +0105
Streams as for Magharee Sound at up to 1.5kn
RNLI Offshore Tyne and inshore lifeboat

The waters from north of the Magharees into Tralee Bay are relatively shallow. There is no promulgated approach to Fenit so study the chart before making a bad weather, night or poor visibility entry. For the best water and to avoid possible breakers keep two miles north of the Magharees, on a westerly heading, to intercept the white sector (bearing 140° - 152°) of Little Samphire lighthouse. 2.2 miles from the light (crossing the 10m depth contour) turn on to a more southerly heading – as it now shallows rapidly to the east of the white sector. Continue past the lighthouse until well into the 5m+ soundings before heading for the quick red on Great Samphire Island, the southwestern corner of the harbour. Bear in mind unmarked drying Wheel Rock west-northwest of Great Samphire Island. Keep in 5–7m outside the floodlit south wall until rounding the 2 fixed reds at the eastern entrance to Fenit's outer commercial harbour. The entrance to the marina is to starboard, marked by Iso.R and Iso.G lights.

FENIT MARINA

If contact with the marina has not been possible take, or raft up on, an outside pontoon. As always you will soon be met and directed to a suitable berth. There is a diesel berth. The excellent facilities are on the north mole of the marina. The marina and harbour

Little Samphire Island from W

offices are here, together with the RNLI boathouse and Fenit Sea Angling Club. There is a security gate and CCTV surveillance. Disabled sailors have a lift for getting on and off a pontoon. Gas is not stocked but the marina manager can organise Camping Gaz. Marina dues can be paid, and euros drawn, by credit card.

Tralee Bay Sailing Club, with splendid quarters overlooking the harbour, may have a visitors' mooring. It is possible to find 3m for anchoring NE of the harbour – clear of commercial shipping. The club has a slip and a drying pontoon and is very welcoming. It holds frequent cruiser races and has a dinghy

SV *Jeanie Johnson* in Fenit Harbour with Slieve Mish Mountains beyond

outside the viaduct is a popular bathing place, so holidaymakers are also catered for. The old station yard has a bottle and can bank. The yard is a good night-stop for motor caravans, with no questions asked!

To revictual completely it is 13km by road to Tralee. A return bus service operates on Wednesdays and Fridays, with a stop near a large SuperValu. It is usually possible to get a lift into Tralee from a marina berth-holder or a member of the Angling Club. For chandlery contact Landers Leisure Lines in Tralee ☎ 066 7126644
Email landers.leisure@oceanfree.net

sailing school. Should many yachts be leaving the marina for a race, or returning, it is best to stand off for awhile.

Large fishing vessels use the harbour and yachts can have fish ice at any time. There is a fresh fish stall, and homely St Brendan Visitor Centre has a café. In 2004 a monument to St Brendan was erected on the summit of Great Samphire Island. This navigating saint was born at Fenit.

Fenit village has a good store with a post office and sells Kos but not wine. There are good pubs serving meals and the beach

TRALEE

The ship canal and turning basin have recently been renovated and a new sea-lock was installed in 2003. In 2004 none of the canal below the bridge was open to shipping – a pity as this could make canal-side access for yachts to this interesting old town. Nor was there anywhere a tender could get alongside Blennerville. The canal has a small marina basin on the outskirts of Tralee, but there are wires over the canal and a closed swing bridge at Blennerville.

The restored Tralee Ship Canal from W. The old quay at Blennerville is just below the white windmill. The replica *Jeanie Johnson* was built in the yard by this quay

As well as being the shopping capital of Kerry, this town by the River Lee chooses the Rose of Tralee annually. In 1840 William Pembroke Mulchinoc penned his song whose first verse ended thus:

'She was lovely and fair as the rose of summer
Yet 'twas not her beauty alone that won me.
On, no! 'Twas the truth in her eyes ever beaming
That made me love Mary, The Rose of Tralee.'

This is an international contest now and the Rose is not necessarily a local colleen.

Another famous lady of Tralee was the SV *Jeanie Johnson*. A three-masted barque, she was built in 1847 for Nicholas Donovan of Tralee for the Atlantic trade. 106ft overall, with a professional crew of 17 she could carry 200 passengers or the equivalent in cargo – for which she was designed. During the Great Famine she carried 2,500 emigrants to Quebec. She was never a 'coffin ship', as were many other unsuitable emigrant ships at that terrible time. Her captain was a Master Mariner and she always carried the same doctor, a fully qualified man who spent his whole working life at sea. *Jeanie* never lost a single passenger through disease. Most of the emigrants she carried were not direct victims of the famine; many were seeking a better way of life and some became prominent citizens in North America. In 1858 the ship foundered while bringing timber from Quebec, but all her crew were rescued by a Dutch brig.

In 1993 it was decided to build a seaworthy replica at Blennerville. An international team of young people, under the guidance of experienced shipwrights, constructed the 500-ton (700 burthen) vessel on a raft. In 2002 she was launched at the disused quay where ships lay alongside before the canal was built. The ground beneath this is in a disgraceful state; it is the tip for every unwanted domestic appliance. It would cost little to make this beautiful stone quay fit for yachts to lie against, or to install a pontoon for tenders. Yacht crews could then take the steam train which shuttles between Blennerville and Tralee. (This narrow gauge railway once ran to Dingle.) Visit the restored working windmill at Blennerville to learn more about the original *Jeanie Johnson* as well as the grinding of corn.

The new *Jeanie* set sail from Fenit for a very successful tour of North America in 2003, riding out storms as bad as any that her famous predecessor encountered. In 2004 she sailed to Spain, then visited many ports

The Pikemen's Monument in Denny Street, Tralee, commemorating the 1798 rebellion

around Ireland with paying passengers. At each port she was opened to visitors. Whilst in harbour this fine vessel was, unfortunately, too often advertised solely as a replica of a famine ship, giving the impression she was an infamous 'coffin ship.'

Though supported by the Irish government, her upkeep has to be met from what she can earn, despite the huge goodwill she has created, especially in North America. Many commentators decry her cost – which was over budget – although this seems surprising for an island nation that has always depended on ships for trade and communication, and still keeps many old ports open for commerce.

The Kerry County Museum in the Ashe Memorial Hall must be visited. Thomas Ashe was a member of the Irish Volunteers who died on hunger strike whilst imprisoned in 1917. This is no jazzy tourist attraction. It stands at the bottom of gracious Denny Street. Besides permanent exhibits on all facets of life in County Kerry, from the Stone Age to the present day, it hosts special exhibitions of international interest. There are many old photographs and fascinating relics on loan from various sources as well as a very realistic recreation of life and trade in the medieval port of Tralee – complete with all the sights, sounds and smells!

Golfers and anglers have already been well catered for in this guide. At Tralee the racing man can enjoy his sport at famous Ballybegan Race Course, on the outskirts of Tralee. The two main annual events are during the Whit weekend in June and the Rose of Tralee Festival in August.

EXCURSIONS FROM FENIT

Northward from Tralee Bay the mountains give way to low-lying limestone country. The seven miles of dunes facing the shallow bay between Fenit and Kerry Head are not for coasting. A sombre grey monument stands

The entrance to Barrow Harbour at LW, from the golf course

behind the strand, 4km north of Fenit Island. The inscription reads: 'At a spot near Banna Strand, adjacent to here, Roger Casement – humanitarian and Irish Revolutionary Leader – Robert Monteith and another man came ashore from a German submarine on Good Friday morning, 21 April 1916, in furthering the cause of Irish Freedom.'

A visit by bicycle over very rough roads through the saltings, returning by Ardfert's religious ruins, is well worthwhile. Collect a freshly-made picnic from the shop when you set out. Fenit Island is kept very private by its farmer and the shores are difficult to scramble along. Drying Barrow Harbour is a haven for wild life, anglers and small boats. It is overlooked by a beautiful 18-hole golf course designed by Arnold Palmer.

BARROW HARBOUR

Situated between the mainland and Fenit Island, this ancient harbour was very heavily defended. Between the island and the golf course there is a deep-water inlet with a beautiful anchorage below Fenit Castle. Tides are strong in the entrance and have carved out ever-changing pools. From attractive Little Samphire Island lighthouse keep well offshore

Barrow harbour at LW. Note the sandbank in the entrance, with round Barrow Castle and the golf course to the right of it. The anchorage is just beyond Fenit Castle

Kerry Head

Banna Strand

Barrow Castle

Golf course

Fenit Castle

Good for picnics

Barrow Harbour's peaceful anchorage beneath Fenit Castle at LW, from the golf course

TIPSY BRADAN

A dish from Ballydavid, Co. Kerry

Bradan is salmon. This recipe can also be used, with your own adaptation, for herrings (*Tipsy Cadan*) and mackerel (*Tipsy Ronnach*)

Ingredients for 4 people
4 salmon fillets
2 medium carrots
2 medium onions (one chopped, one sliced)
1 clove garlic
2tsp parsley (dried or fresh)
4 black peppercorns (if available, otherwise increase amount of seasoning)
3 cloves (or ½tsp ground cloves)
1tsp dried thyme
1tsp salt & pepper mixed
1tbsp vinegar
1 pint Irish stout
½ pint light ale
(In this traditional recipe we find the suggested liquid is too much. Add to taste and desired consistency. Also, as Irish leeks are so good we usually replace the onions with these.)

To cook
Mix together chopped carrots, chopped leek, garlic, herbs, spice and seasoning. Pour in the stout and simmer until vegetables are cooked. Put into a large oven dish, place the fish on top, pushing the fillets well into the vegetables, and cover with the finely sliced leek rings. Pour in vinegar and light ale. Cover loosely with foil. Bake in a moderate to hot oven for 20-30 minutes (fish should have just reached the 'flaking' stage). Serve with freshly made soda bread. This dish is sometimes served cold.

to round the reef and shallows off the island, then head northwest of The Rose to positively identify Illaunnacusha. This is left close to starboard, with a drying spit of sand to port. Locals 'driving' round from Fenit keep south of Illaunnacusha then turn tightly around the larger inner reef. This is just an islet at high water, opposite the round tower of Barrow Castle on the mainland. As usual, *Balair* came in just after LW slack when the sharp-edged sand bar just inside the entrance was showing, as was most of the reef extending out to the islet. The photographs and plan show all this well. Track was then southwesterly before following the curve of the bay to starboard in 1.5m to 2m. It was deeper but streamy beyond Fenit Castle but *Balair* found good comfortable holding in 1.5m over the anchor on the plan. A family of choughs fluttered around the water's edge castle whilst *Balair* swung easily, within half a cable of rocks and sand at low water. An angler came alongside in his boat to offer a bass: *Balair* was the first yacht he had ever seen in this peaceful sheltered spot.

Tarbert Island in the Shannon estuary. There is a vehicle ferry to Kilrush, in County Clare, which has a marina. This is convenient for crews flying into Shannon. Both harbours are described in ISDs

Anchorage

To Tarbert

APPENDIX

AVAILABILITY OF FACILITIES FOR EACH CRUISING AREA

The cruising sailor is well provided for in the areas described in Sections 1 and 2 but proceeding north and west facilities become fewer and far between. To arrive, say, in the Kenmare River without adequate fuel, water and victuals would be very unfortunate. The following list should ensure that this does not happen.

Limited victuals are obtainable from other harbours, as mentioned in the text. Camping Gaz is often out of stock. Most touring caravan and camping sites stock it.

	Green diesel	Alongside water (non-marina)	Marinas & pontoons	Visitors' moorings	Supermarkets	Showers (non-marina)	Camping Gaz
Area 1							
Youghal	•	•			•		•
Crosshaven	•	•	•	•	•		•
East Ferry	•		•				
Kinsale	•		•	•	•		•
Cóbh			•		•		•
Ballycotton		•		•			
Cork City					•		•
Carrigaline					•		
Midleton					•		•
Area 2							
Courtmacsherry	•	•	•	•			
Union Hall	•	•				•	•
Baltimore	•	•	•			•	•
Clear Island	•	•					
Crookhaven	•	•		•		•	•
Sherkin Island		•	•				
Oldcourt		•	•				
Glandore				•		•	
Schull	•			•	•	•	•
Clonakilty					•		•
Skibbereen					•		•
Area 3							
Castletownbere	•				•	•	•
Lawrence Cove Marina	•		•	•			
Bantry	•	•			•	•	•
Glengarriff		•			•	•	
Adrigole	•	•			•	•	•
Trafrask Bay				•			
Bear Island (Rerrin)							•
Area 4							
Cahersiveen	•	•	•		•		•
Sneem		•		•			•
Dunkerron		•					
Kenmare		•			•		•
Portmagee		•		•		•	
Valentia		•		•			
Darryname		•					
Area 5							
Dingle	•		•		•		•
Fenit	•		•		•		•
Kells Bay				•			

BAREBOAT CHARTER

CORK

Yacht Harbour Management berth a fully-equipped fleet of yachts for bareboat charter at East Ferry. Crews can be collected from the airport or ferry to take over in Cork or Kinsale.
☎ 021 481 3911 *Fax* 021 481 3916
Email jor@emeraldislegroup.ie
ww.sailcorkharbour.com

KINSALE

Sail Ireland, based at the Trident Hotel Marina, Kinsale, have a fleet of fully-equipped modern yachts for bareboat charter.
☎ 021 477 2927 *Fax* 021 477 4170
Email info@sailireland.com www.sailireland.com

VALENTIA

10° West (Moody S31, with a larger boat planned).
☎ 066 947 2244 Mobile 0872 600748
Email andrew@qcbar.com
www.yachtcharterkerry.com

SELF-DRIVE CAR HIRE

Minimum age 23, having held a driving licence for 3 years. All international Car Hire companies can be found.

COBH AND CORK

Great Island Car Rentals Rushbrooke, Cóbh, Co. Cork and 47 MacCurtain Street, Cork will deliver long and short-term self-drive cars anywhere in Cork and Kerry. Their brochure has a lot of information on all forms of travel to and in Munster.
☎ 021 481 1609/021 459 3536 *Fax* 021 481 3181
Email greatislandcarrentals@hotmail.com

BANTRY

Berry's of Bantry
☎ 027 50589

Sneem Car Rentals
www.budget.com

MARINE SERVICES

Chandlers
CORK

Union Chandlery, 4-5 Penrose Quay, Cork City
☎ 021 455 4334 *Fax* 021 455 2211
Email sales@unionchandlery.com
www.unionchandlery.com

SKIBBEREEN

CH Marine Ltd, Nautic House, Marsh Road Industrial Estate, Skibbereen, Co. Cork
☎ 028 23190 *Fax* 028 22028
and at Frankfield Industrial Estate, Cork City
☎ 021 431 5700 *Fax* 021 431 6160
Email sales@chmarine.com
www.chmarine.com

Ireland has no discount chandlers, but both these concerns have large showrooms and stock almost every item of chandlery for fishing vessels and yachts, available by mail order. Both companies will send an engineer with parts promptly. From experience this is a very efficient service.

Electronic repairs and services
Dunmast Ltd, Mill Road, Kennedy Quay, Cork. They will send a technician with spares.

☎ 021 431 8400 *Fax* 021 431 8500
Email dunmast@tinet.ie
www.homepage.tinet.ie

Engineer (motor yachts)
PowerBoat.Com, Cork
☎ 0857 272382
Email rob@powerboatdoc.com www.powerboatdoc.com

Engineer (sailing yachts)
Salve Marine, Crosshaven
☎021 483 1145 Mobile 0862 601755

Outboard motors and ribs
Marine Motors Ltd, Unit 1, Old Industrial Estate, Little Island, Co. Cork
☎/Fax 021 435 4217
Email email@marinemotorscork.com
www.marinemotorscork.com

Starter motor and alternator repairs
David O'Brien, Midleton, Cork
☎ 021 463 3454 Mobile 0868 456989

Life-rafts
CH Marine (see above) and Midleton Marine Ltd will collect and service life-rafts.
Midleton Marine, Carrigtohill (near Cork)
☎ 021 488 3637 Mobile ☎ 0862 724285/0862 596214
Fax 021 488 3553 *Email* gordon@midletonmarine.com

Sailmaker
Des McWilliam, Crosshaven
☎ 021 483 1505 *Fax* 021 483 1700
Email ukireland@sailmakers.com

CHARTS, MAPS, PILOTS AND NAUTICAL PUBLICATIONS

Charts, almanacs and publications are available from **Imray, Laurie, Norie & Wilson Ltd**, Wych House, The Broadway, St Ives, Cambs PE 27 5BT England
☎ 01480 462114 Fax 01480 496109
Email orders@imray.comwww.imray.com
OSI maps from Imray or from
Ordnance Survey Ireland, Phoenix Park, Dublin 8
☎ 01 802 5300 *Fax* 01 822 0979
Email mapsales@osi.ie
www.osi.ie

RTÉ ALTERNATIVE/DEDICATED FM FREQUENCIES

	Radio 1	*Lyric*
Bantry	88.7	98.3
Cahersiveen	89.5	99.1
Castletownbere	88.3	97.9
Cork	89.7	99.3
Crosshaven	88.2	97.8
Dungarvan	88.5	98.1
Kinsale	89.0	98.6
Smerwick	89.1	98.7
Fenit	88.4	98.0

Further information: www.rte.ie

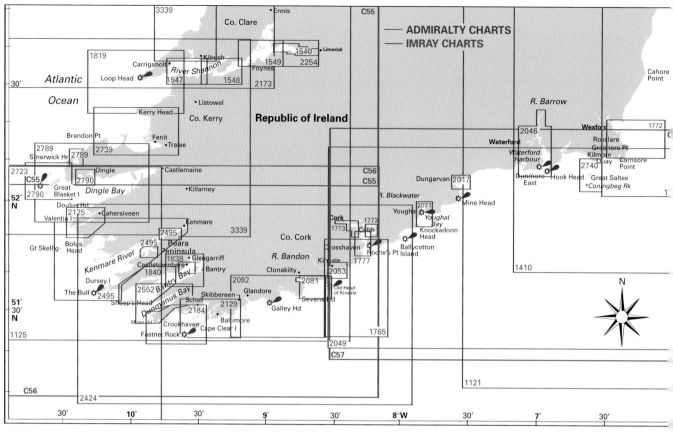

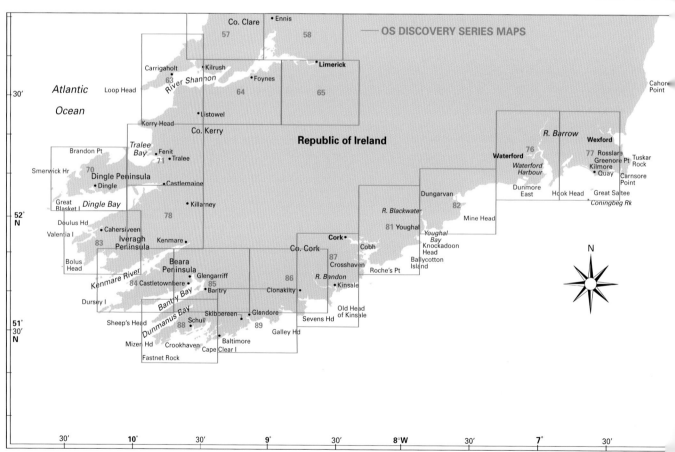

TOURING CARAVAN SITES

See text for good sites used by author.
Full details from:
Irish Caravan & Camping Council, PO Box 4443, Dublin 2
www.camping-ireland.ie

USEFUL CONTACTS

Commissioners of Irish Lights
16 Lower Pembroke Street, Dublin 2
☎ 01 662 4525 *Fax* 01 661 8094
Email cil@aol.ie
www.cil@aol.ie

Department of Communications, Marine and Natural Resources
Leeson Lane, Dublin 2
www.dcmnr.gov.ie

Irish Coast Guard (IRCG)
Dept of Communications, Marine & Natural Resources, Leeson Lane, Dublin 2
☎ 01 619 9349 *Fax* 01 676 2666
Email admin@irishcoastguard.ie
www.dcmnr.gov.ie

Valentia (MRSC)
Emergency: 112 or 999
International: +353 66 947 6109
Email mrscvalentia@irishcoastguard.ie.

Irish Cruising Club
Email publications@irishcruisingclub.com
www.irishcruisingclub.com

ISDs SW Ireland
John Petch, Seaview Farm, Kilbrittain, Co. Cork
☎ 023 49610
johnpetch@eircom.net

Irish Tourist Board
150 New Bond Street, London W1S 2AQ
☎ 0171 518 0800 *Fax* 0171 493 9065
Email via www.ireland.travel.ie

Met Éireann, Glasnevin Hill, Dublin 9
☎ 01 806 4200 Fax 01 806 4247
Email met.eireann@met.ie
www.eireann.ie
Sea area and general forecasts.

United Kingdom Hydrographic Office
Admiralty Way, Taunton, Somerset TA21 2DN
☎ 01823 337900 *Fax* 01823 284077
Email helpdesk@ukho.gov.uk
www.hydro.gov.uk

RECOMMENDED BOOKS

(Some are out of print but may be available from British and Irish Libraries.)
Routard Ireland (Hachette UK) 2000. The best general guide for travellers
Ireland – The Rough Guide (Rough Guides). Also a good general guide
Wild Ireland Brendan Lehane (Sheldrake Press 2000). Good on Cork and Kerry.
The Coast of West Cork Peter Somerville-Large 1972
Cork & Kerry Sean Jennett (Batsford 1977)

Cruising in British and Irish Waters John Watney (David & Charles 1983)
The Brendan Voyage Tim Severin (Hutchinson & Co 1978 and Arrow Books Ltd)
Celtic Gold travel writer/sailor Peter Marshall (Sinclair-Stevenson 1997)
Oileán – A Guide to the Irish Islands David Walsh (Pesda Press 2004)
The Dingle Peninsula: History, Folklore, Archaeology Steve MacDonough (Brandon Book Publishers Ltd, Dingle, Co Kerry)
The Blasket Islands Joan & Ray Stagles (The O'Brien Press, Dublin 1980)
The Most Complete Field Guide to the Birds of Britain and Europe Lars Svenson & Peter Grant (HarperCollins 2002). Excellent illustrations.
Signor Marconi's Magic Box Gavin Weightman (HarperCollins 2003)
Somerville and Ross Gifford Lewis (Penguin 1985)
The Stone Circles of Cork & Kerry Jack Roberts (Bandia 1990). From some Tourist Information Centres
Valentia. A Different Irish Island Nellie O'Cleirigh (Portobello Press, Dublin 1992)
The Skellig Story Des Lavelle (The O'Brien Press, Dublin 1976, updated 1993)
A Concise History of Ireland Máire and Conor Cruise O'Brien (Thames and Hudson, 1985)
The Troubles Ulick O'Connor (Mandarin 1975)
Caravan & Camping Ireland (published annually by the Irish Caravan & Camping Council). €5 from PO Box 4443, Dublin 2, Republic of Ireland
Email info@campingireland.ie.
The Irish Skipper, the Journal of the Irish Fishing Industry, is available monthly from bookstalls in fishing ports. It has much of interest to cruising yachtsmen.
Sherkin Comment is an environmental quarterly from Sherkin Island Marine Station. Details of this and other publications via: www.homepage.eircom.net.
East Cork Area Guide
Cork Area Guide
Kinsale Area Guide
West Cork and Lee Valley Area Guide
Ring of Kerry Area Guide
Dingle Peninsula Area Guide
West Cork Garden Trail
All include a good map and are available at little or no cost from:
Cork Kerry Tourism, Aras Fáilte, Grand Parade, Cork ☎ 021 4273 251
Fax 021 4273 504
Email info@corkkerrytourism.ie
www.corkkerry.ie

INDEX